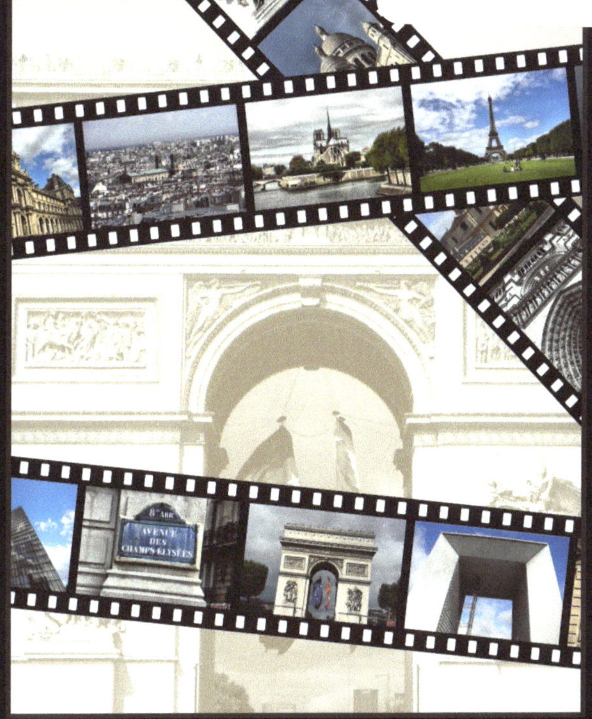

best pictures of

PARIS

Best Pictures of Paris
by Christian Radulescu

ISBN 978-0-9866004-8-7

Printed in the United States of America

Other Books in the Series

- Best Pictures of Rome
- Best Pictures of New York City
- Best Pictures of Chicago
- Best Pictures of London
- Best Pictures of Washington
- Best Pictures of Barcelona
- Best Pictures of Berlin
- Best Pictures of Madrid
- Best Pictures of Boston

Other titles are in preparation.

THE EIFFEL TOWER

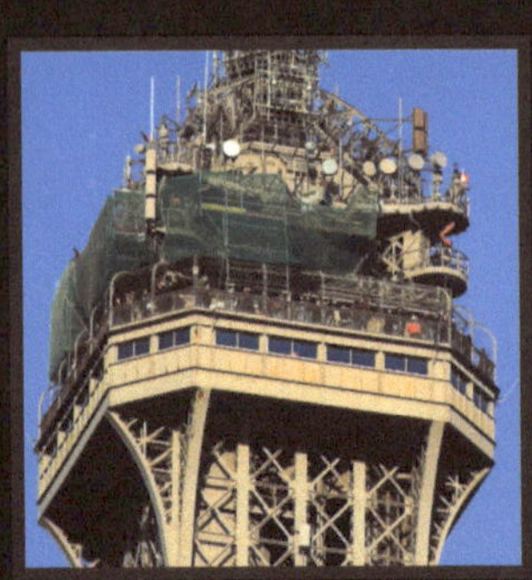

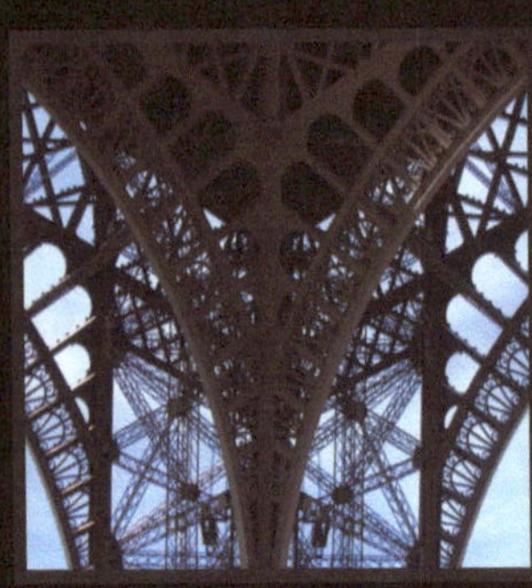

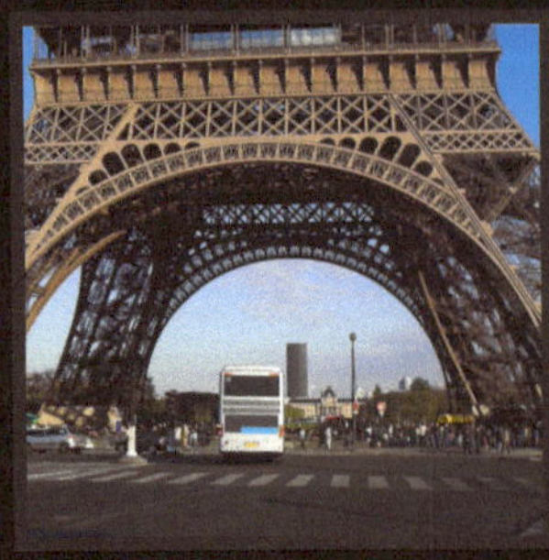

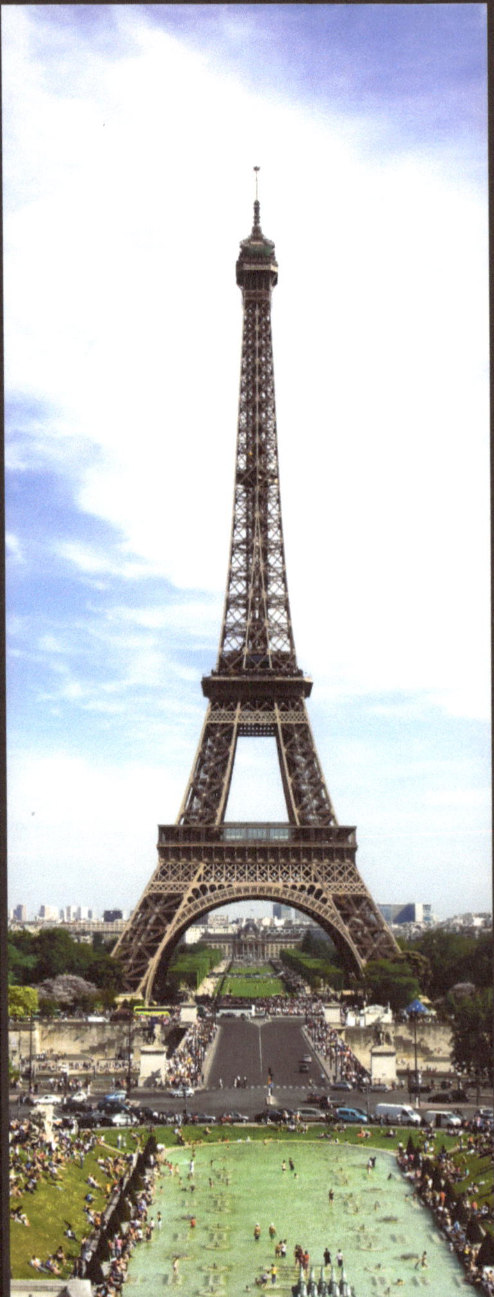

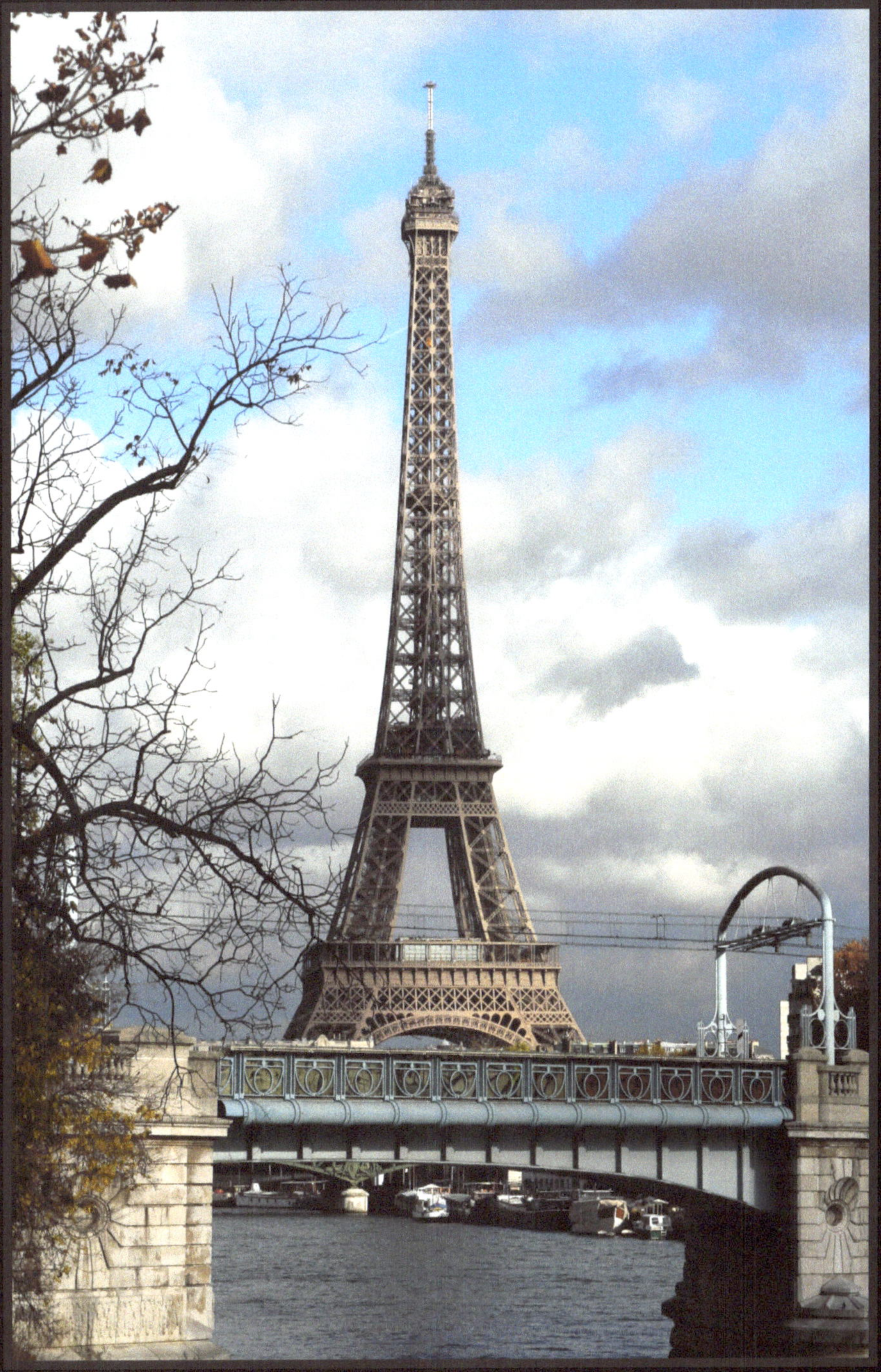

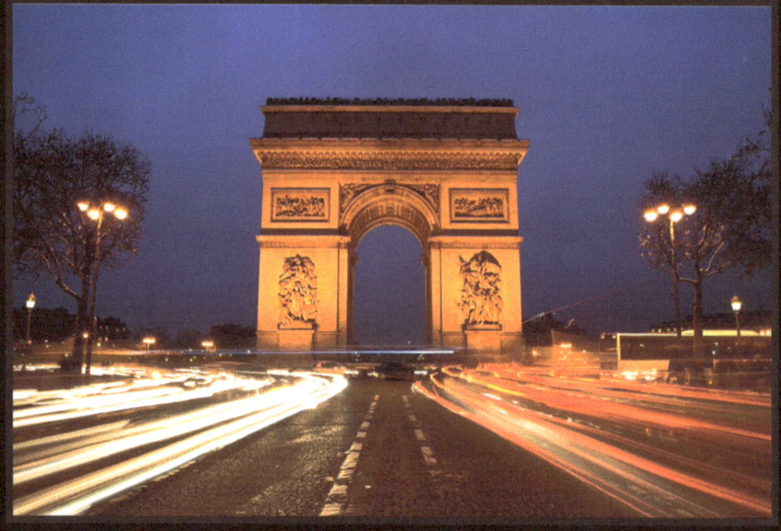

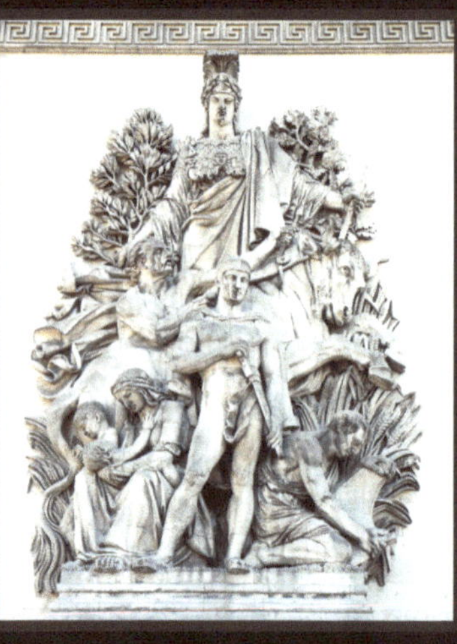

Arc de Triomphe

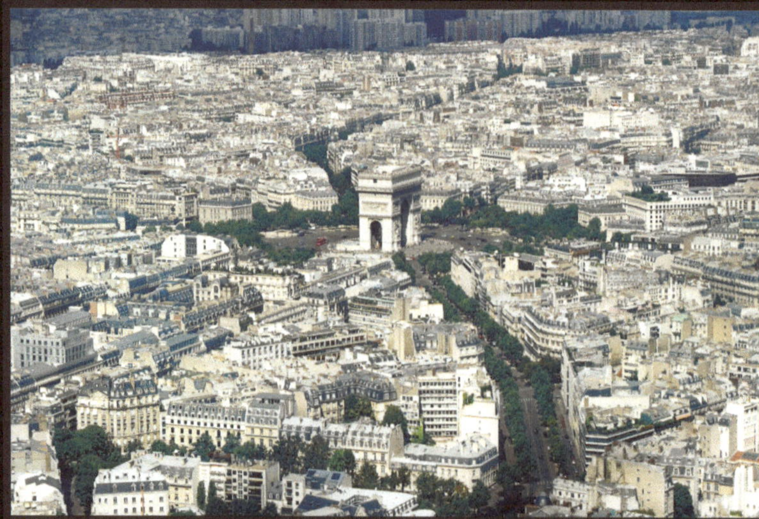

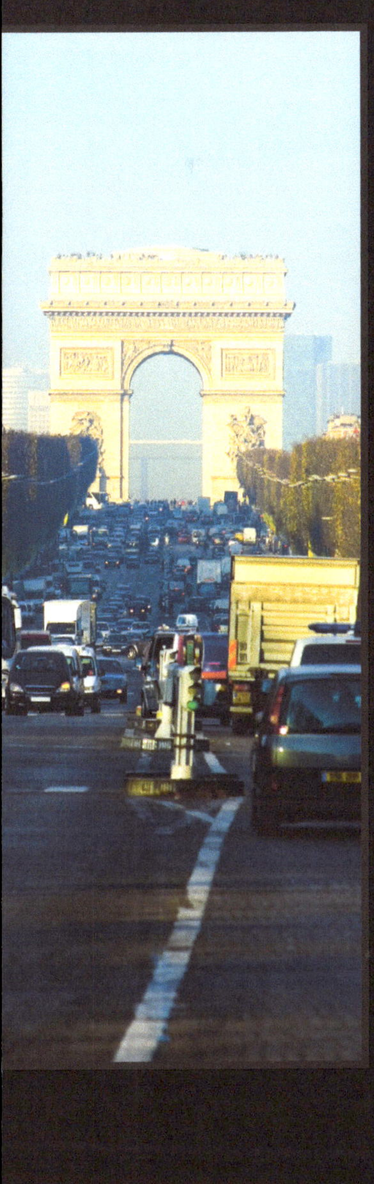

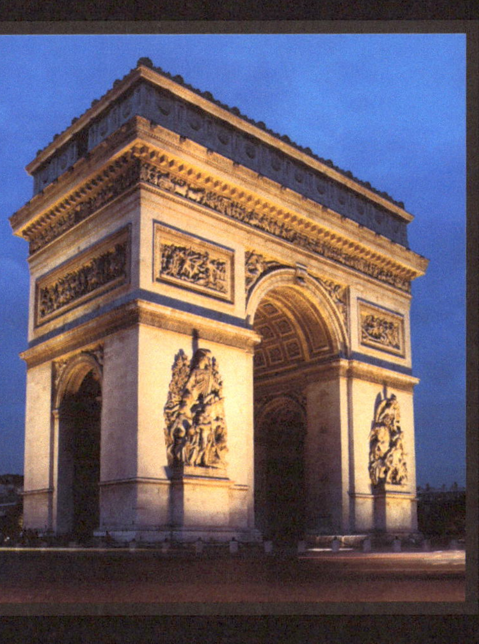

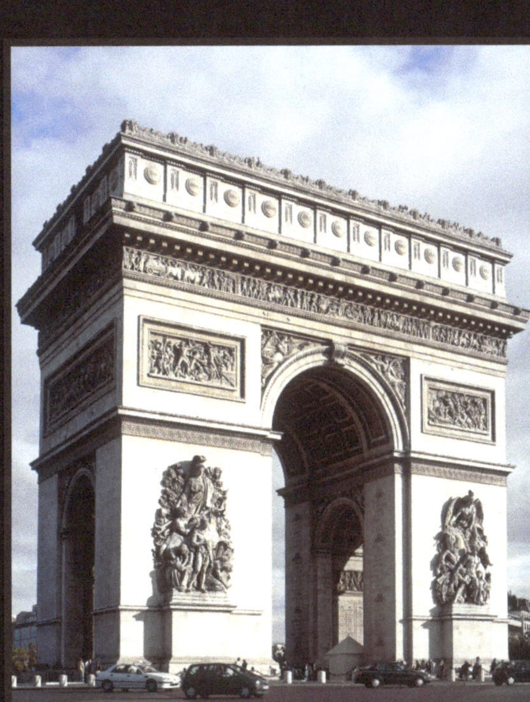

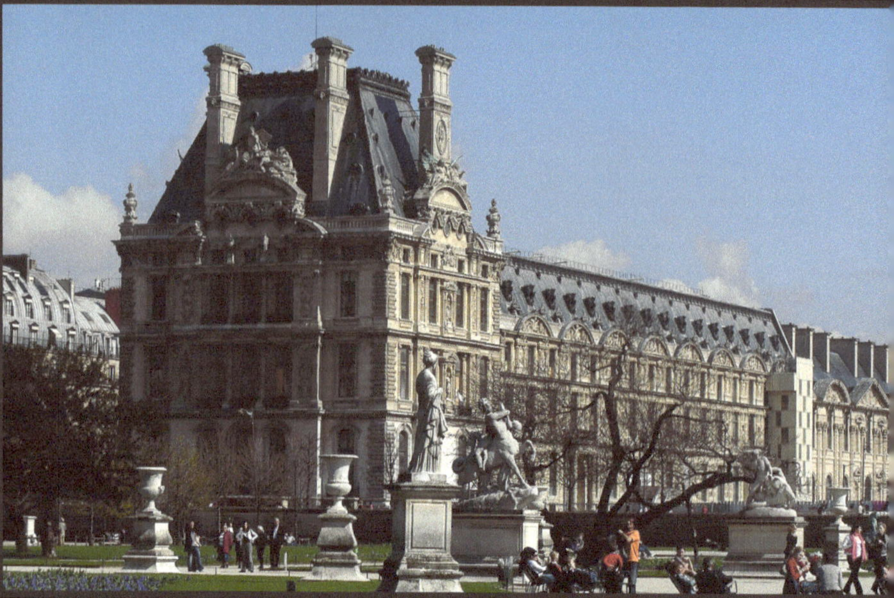

LOUVRE MUSEUM

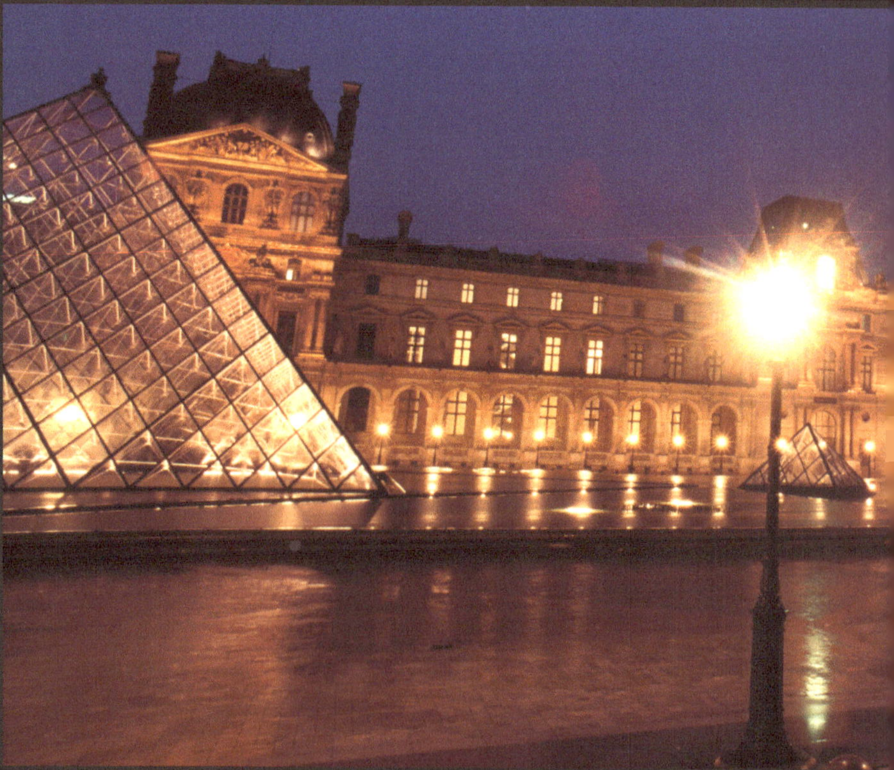

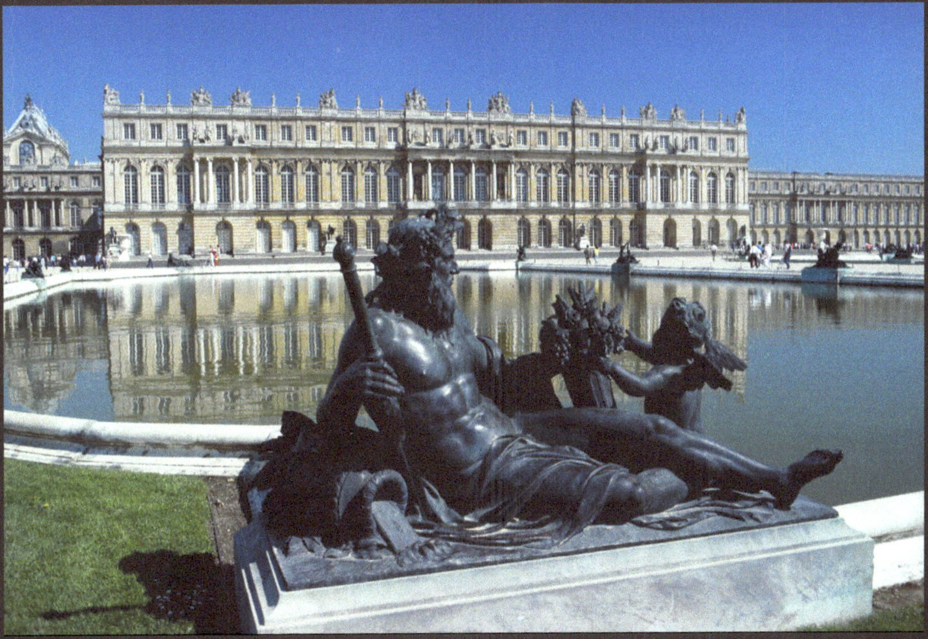

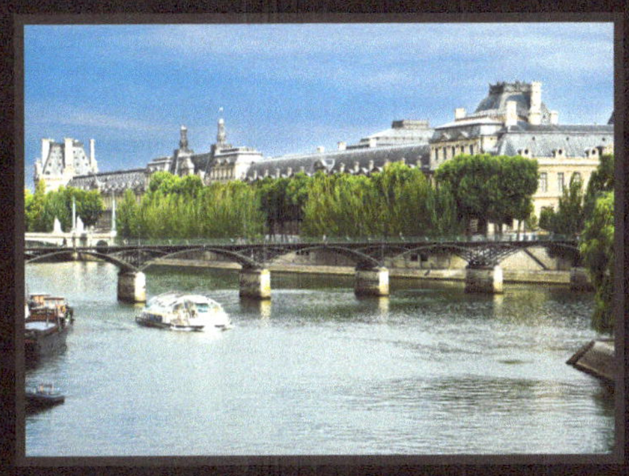

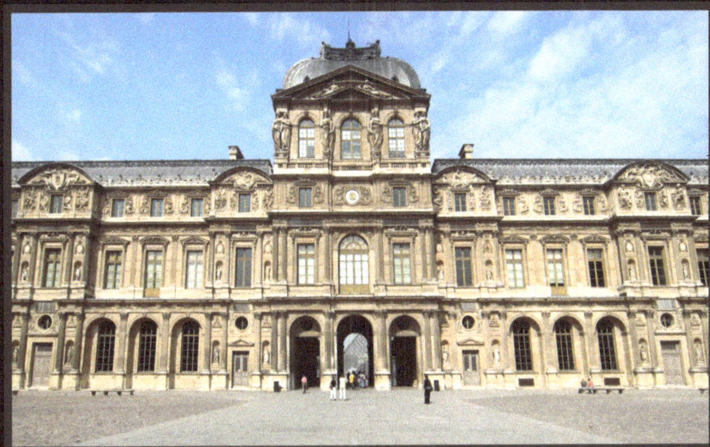

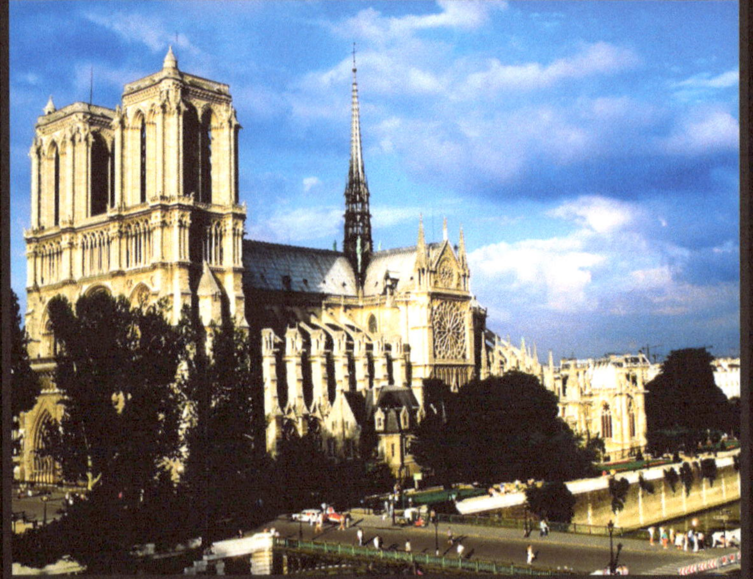

Notre Dame Cathedral

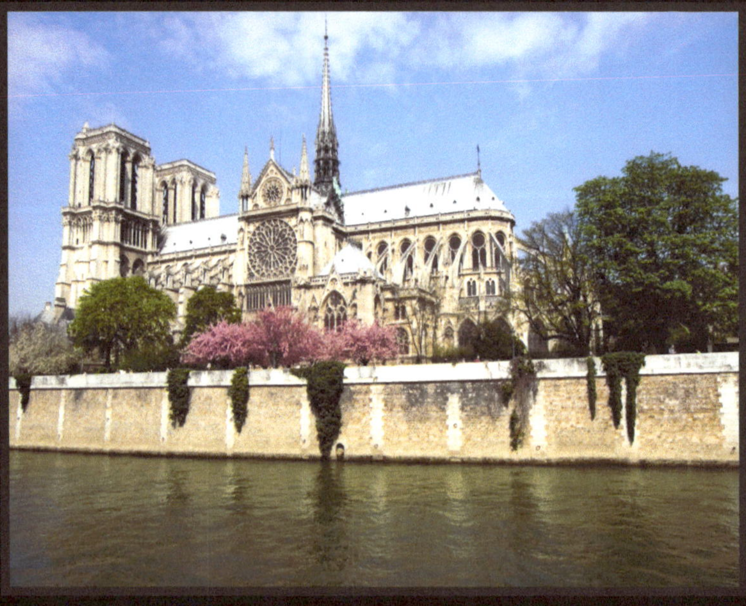

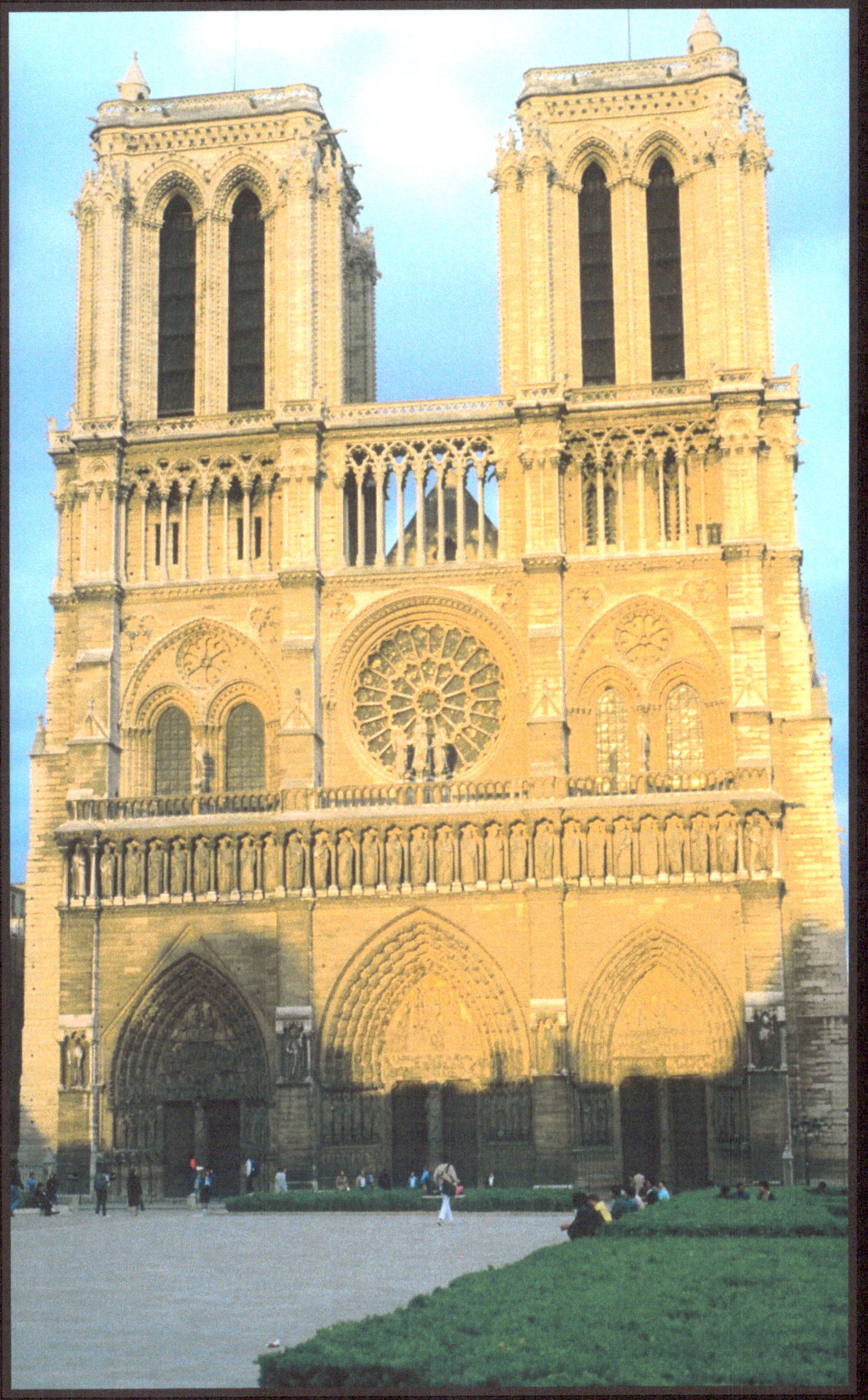

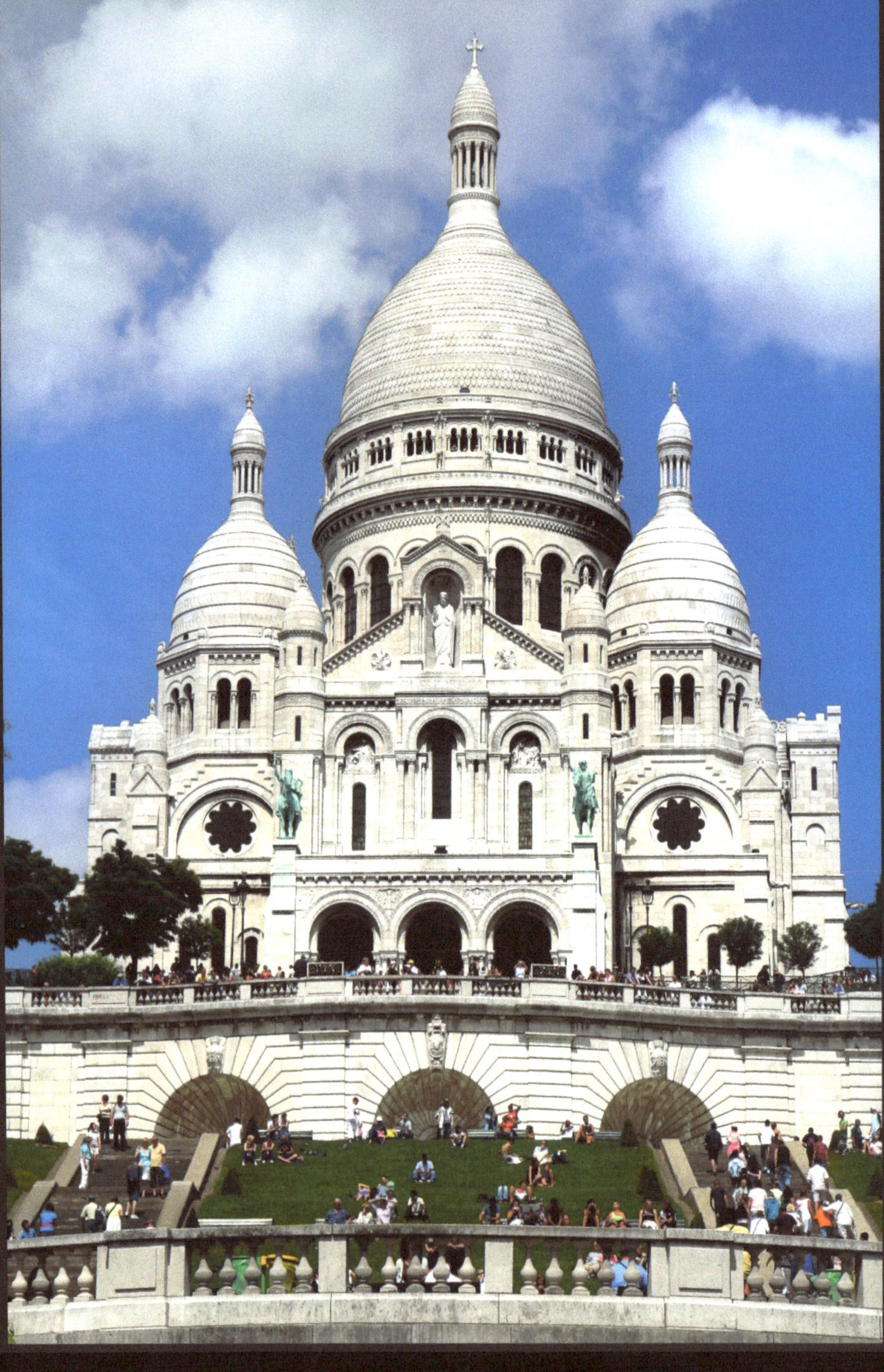

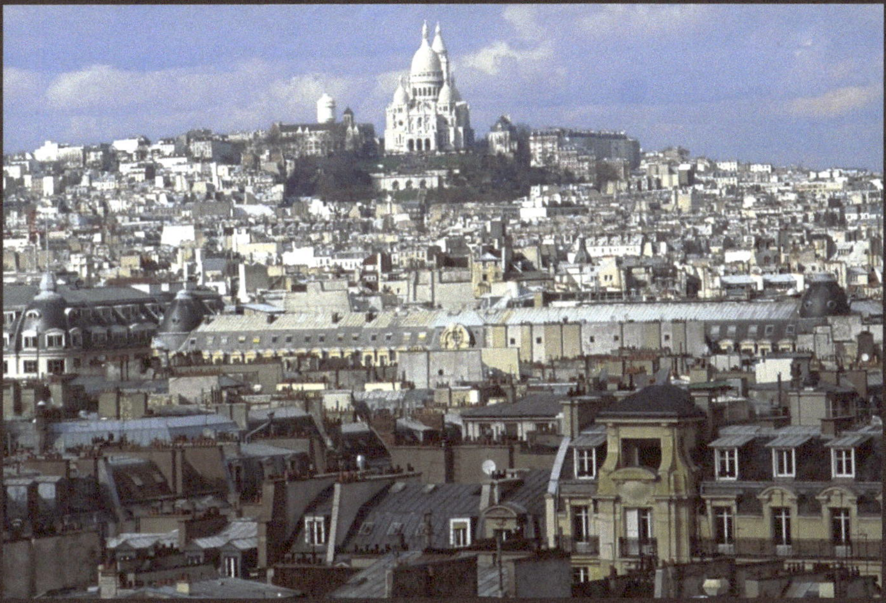

Sacré-Coeur Basilica

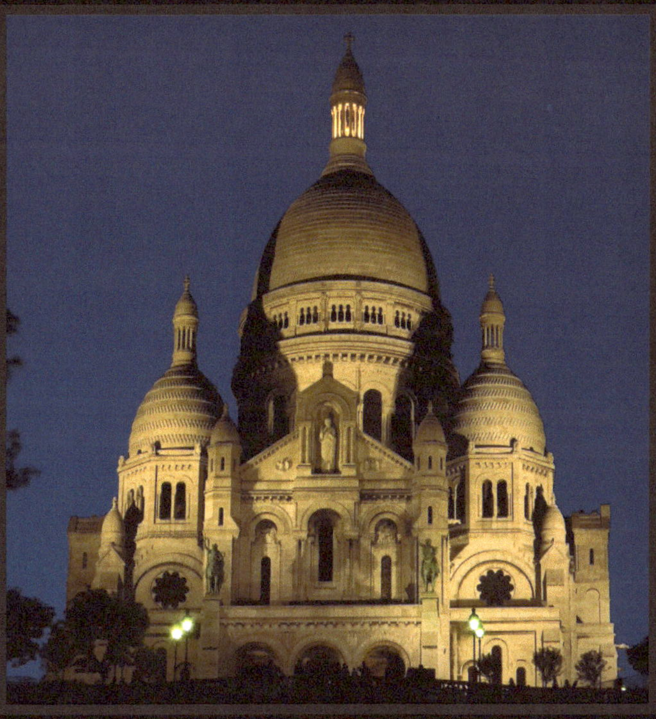

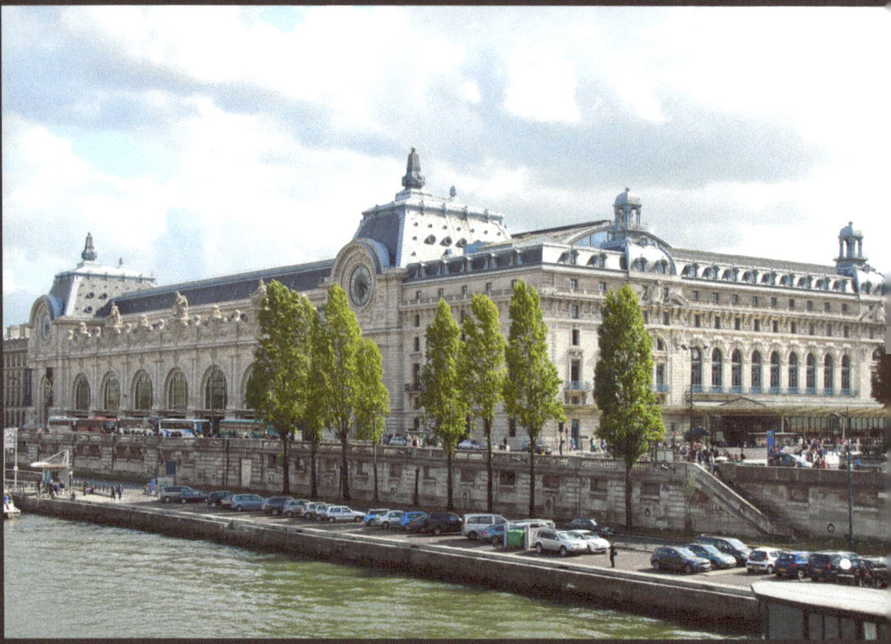

THE ORSAY MUSEUM

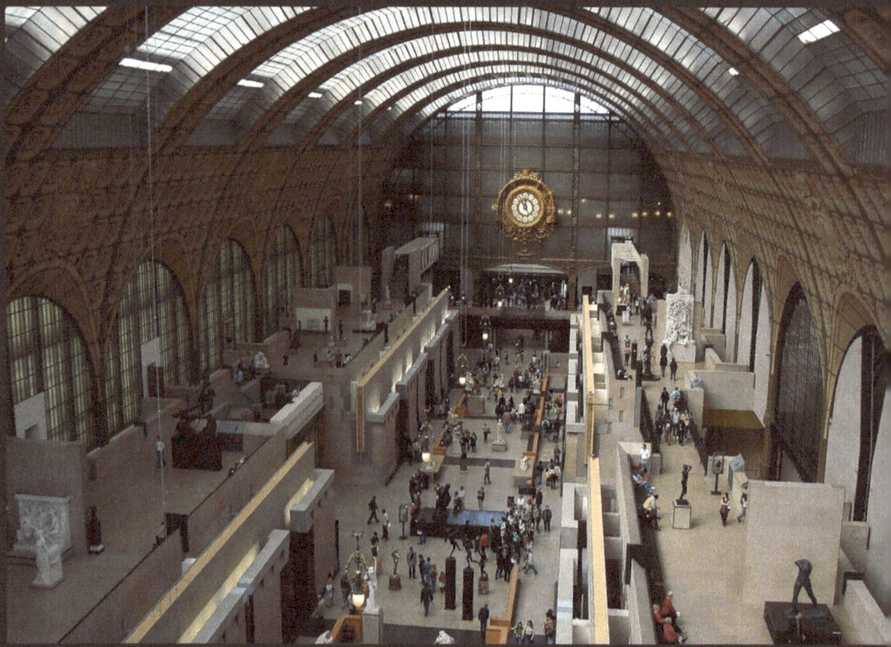

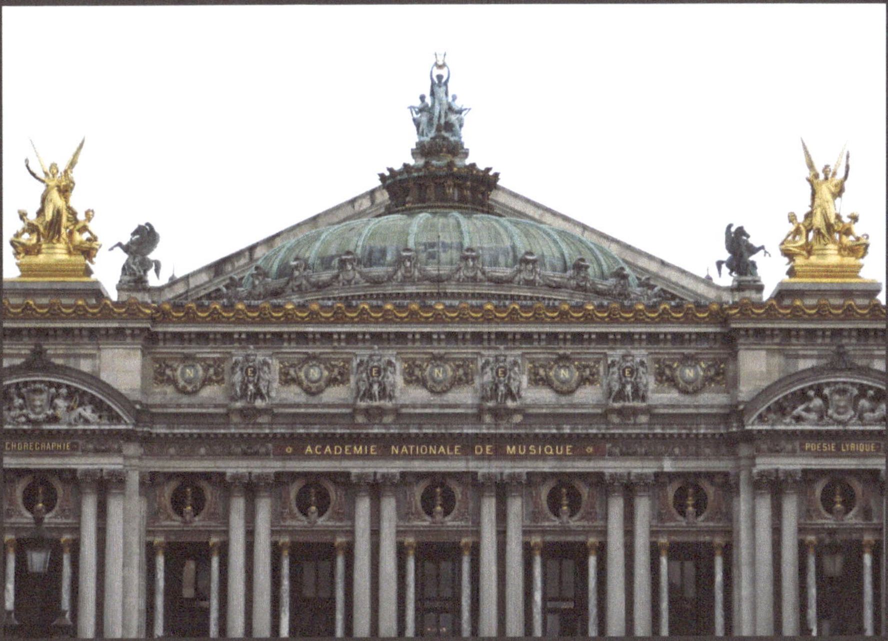

Opera Garnier

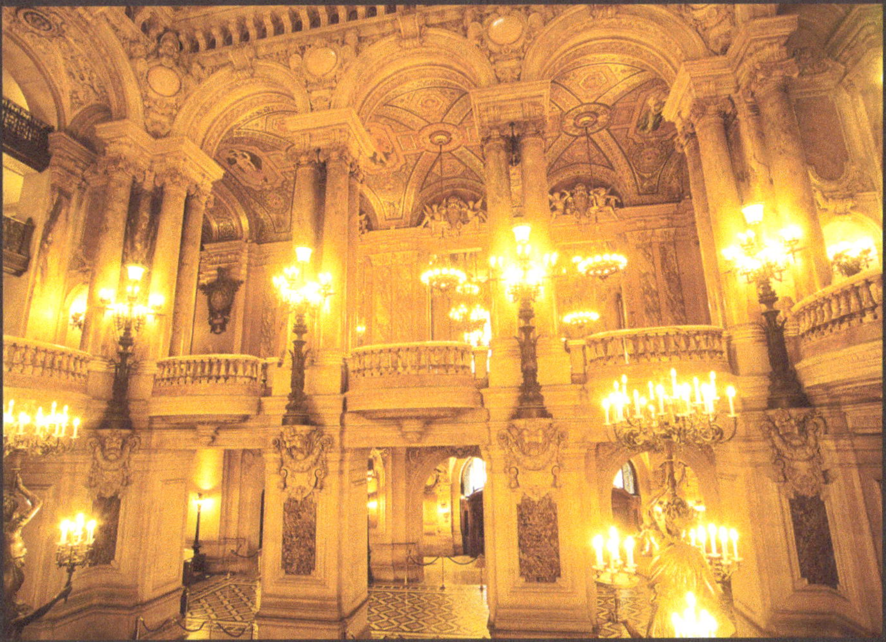

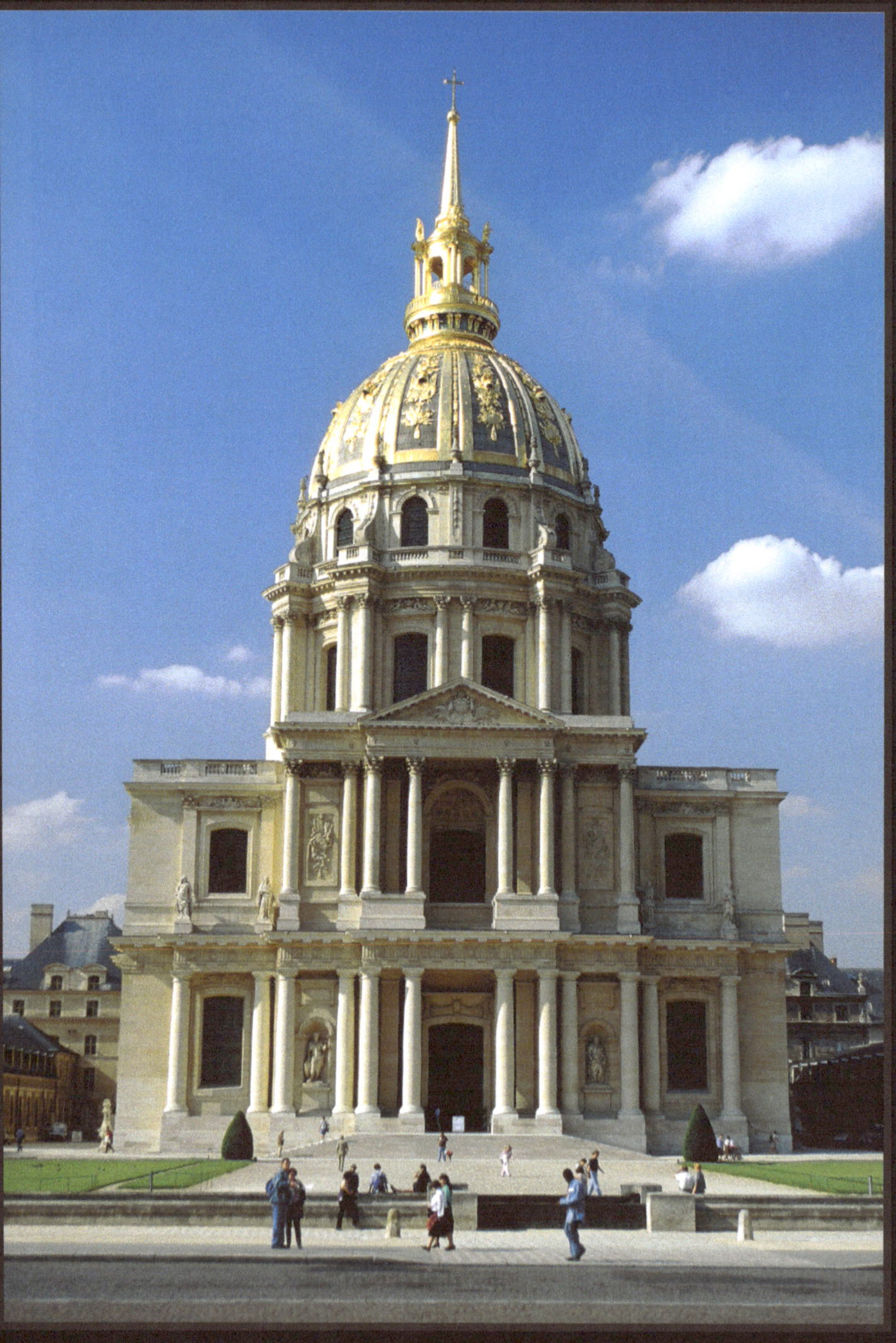

Les Invalides

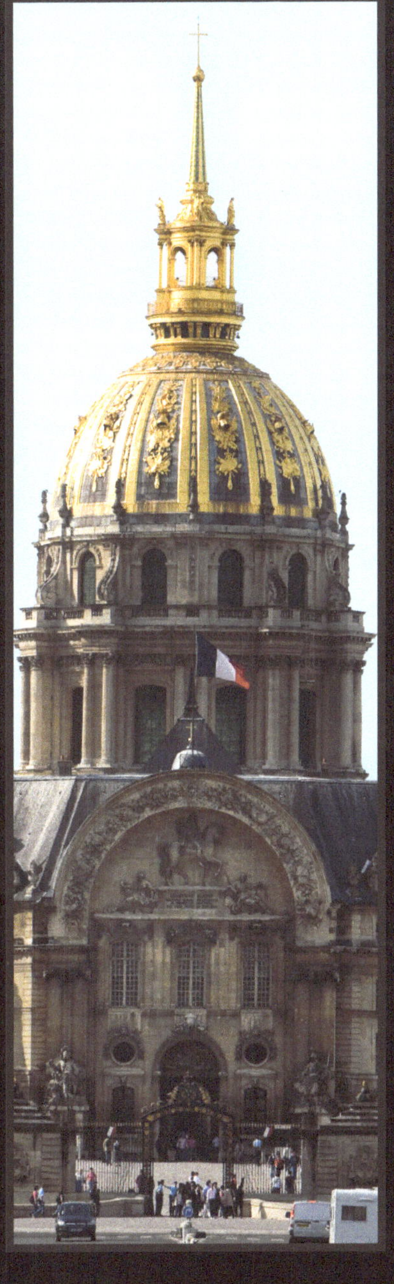
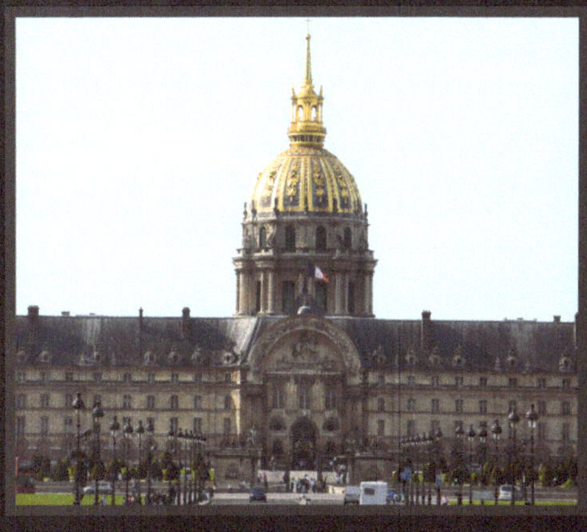
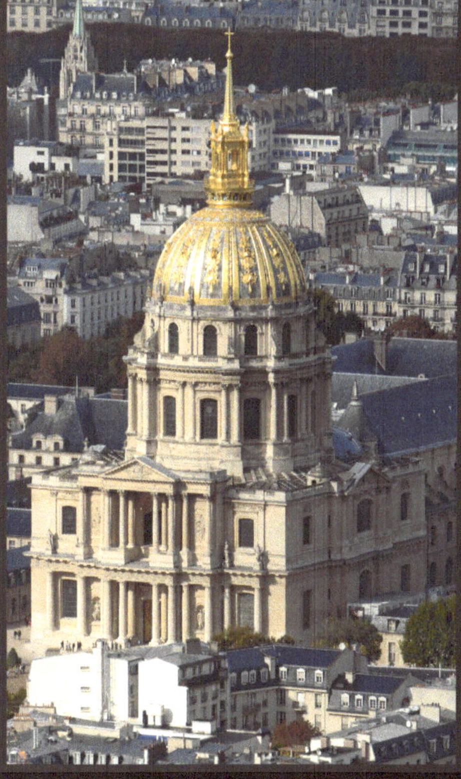

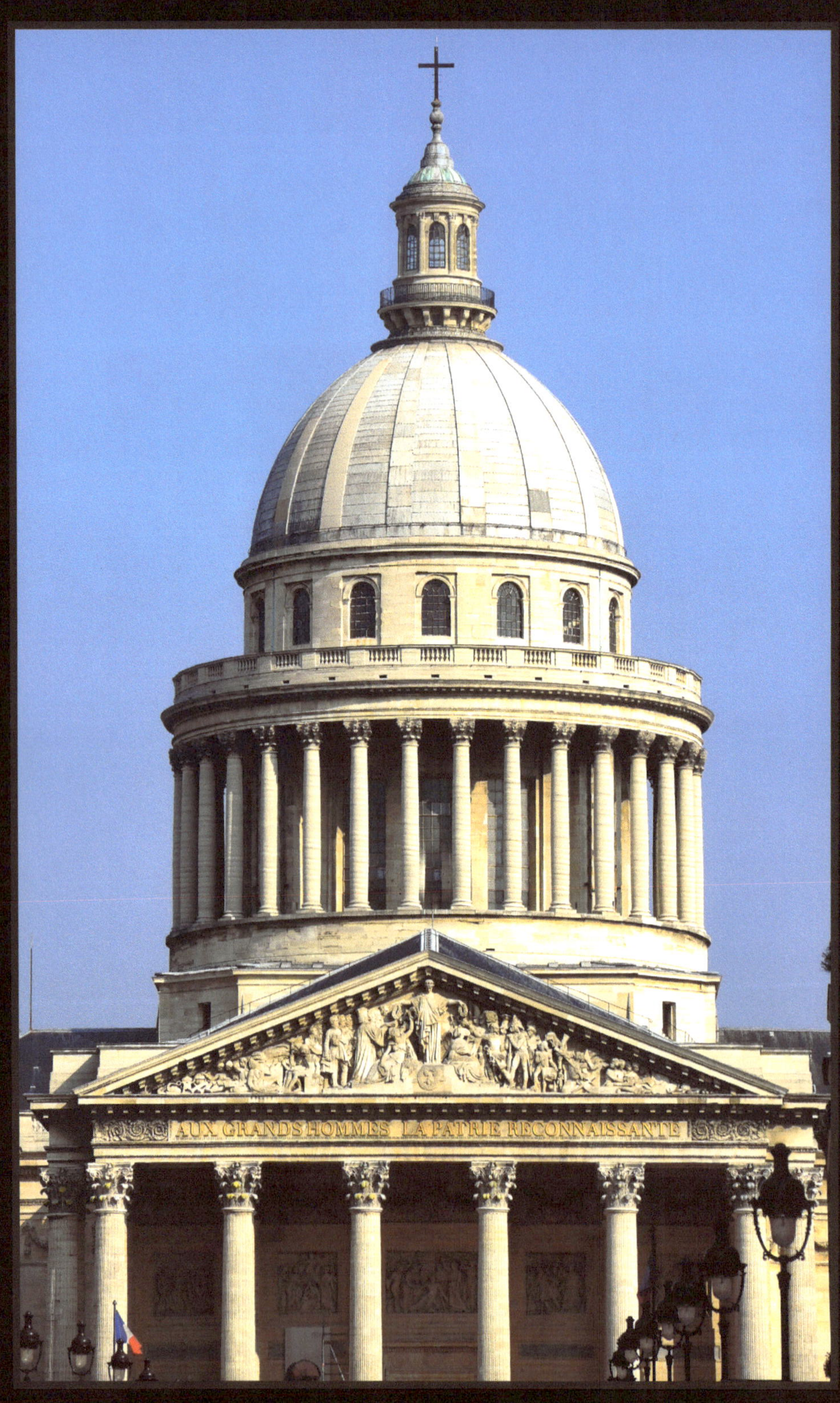
AUX GRANDS HOMMES LA PATRIE RECONNAISSANTE

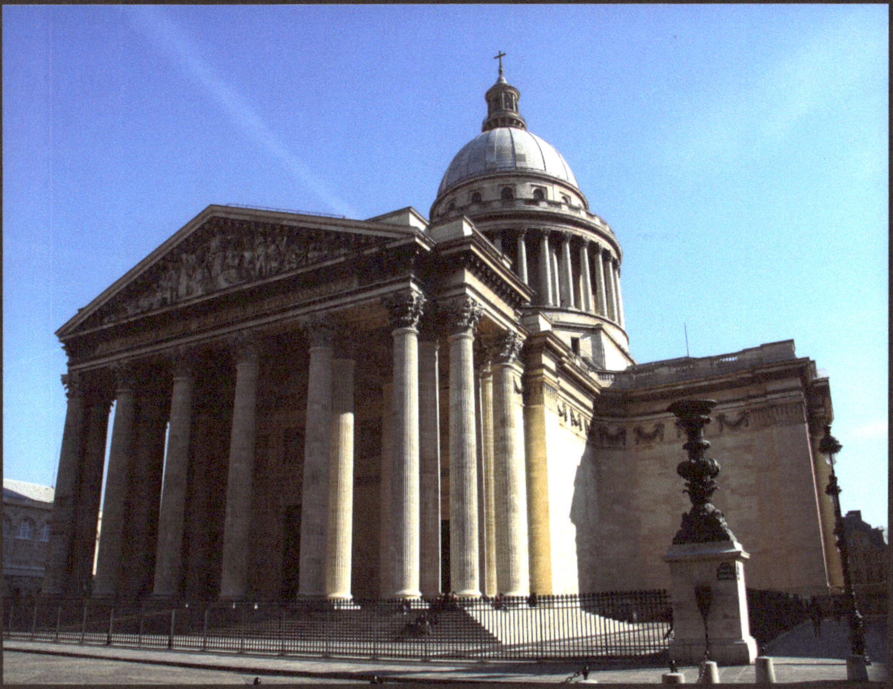

THE PANTHEON

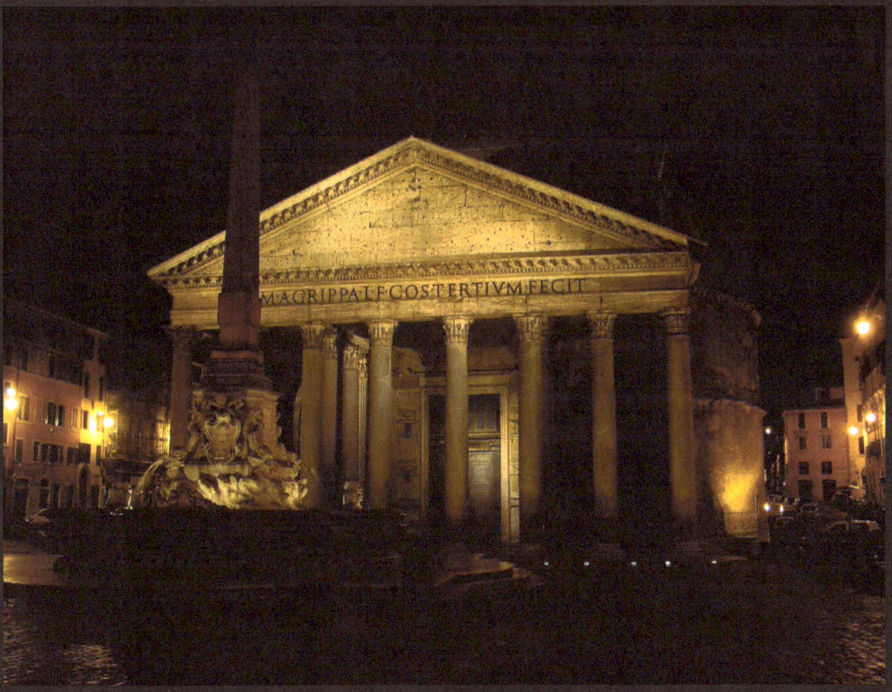

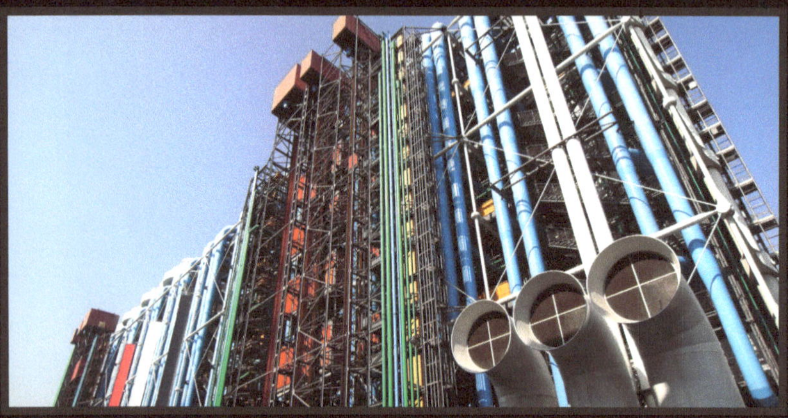

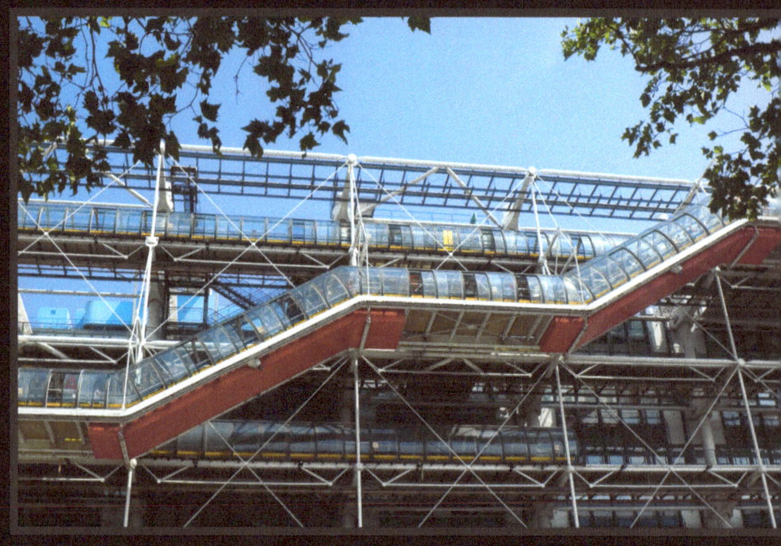

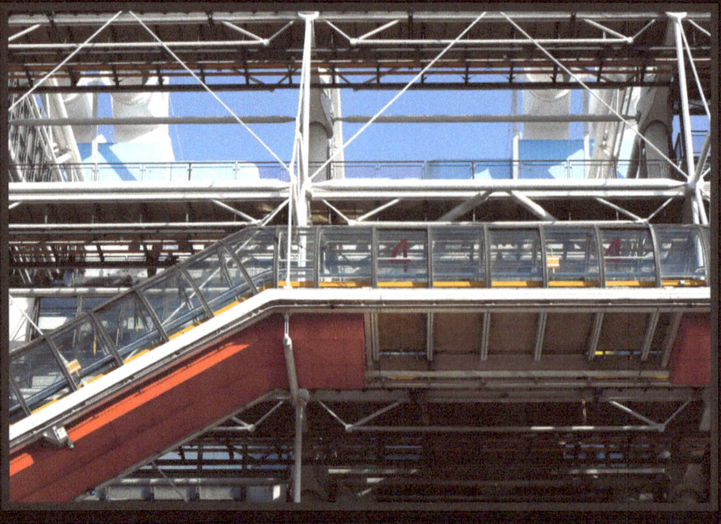
4
4

Pompidou Museum

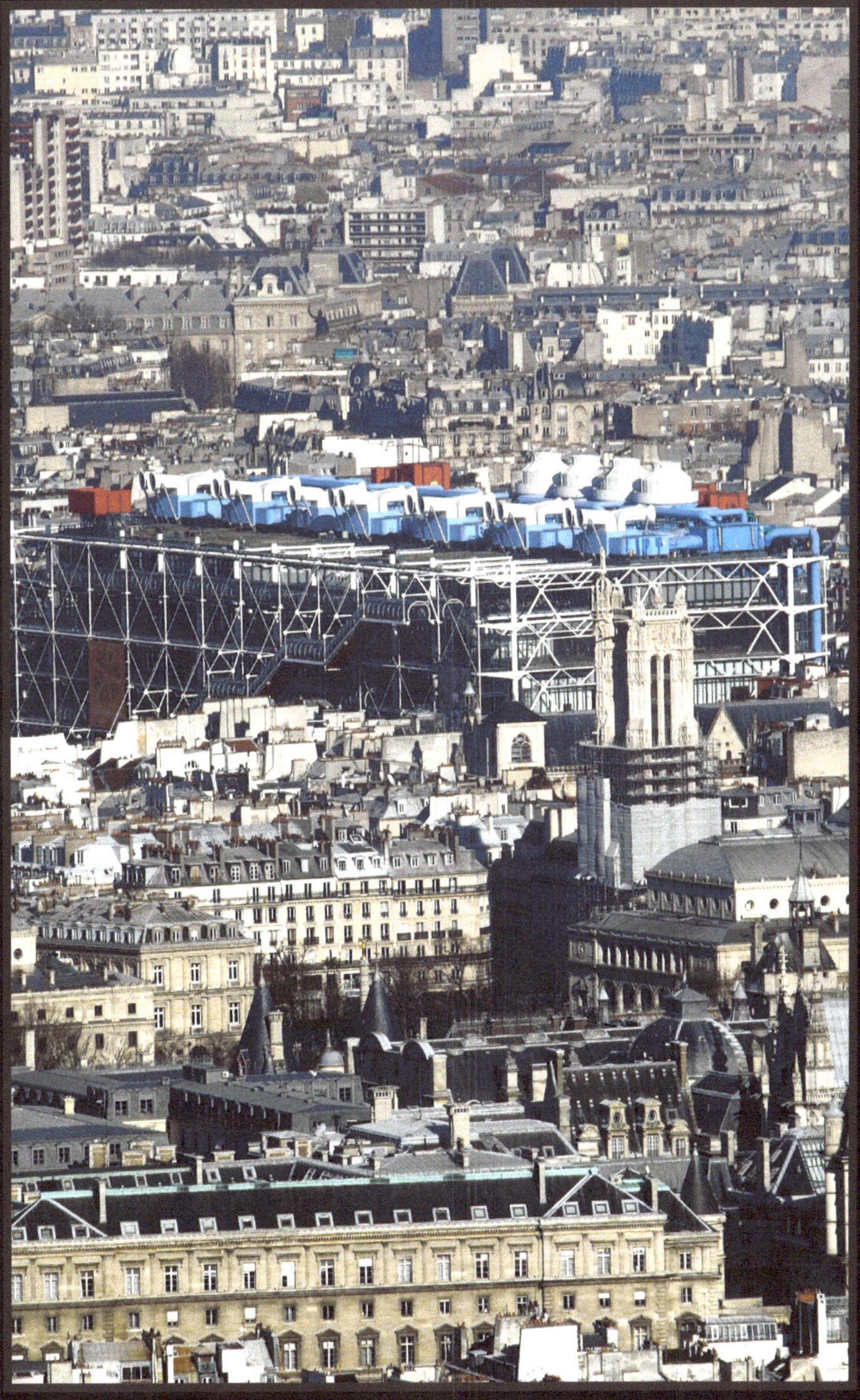

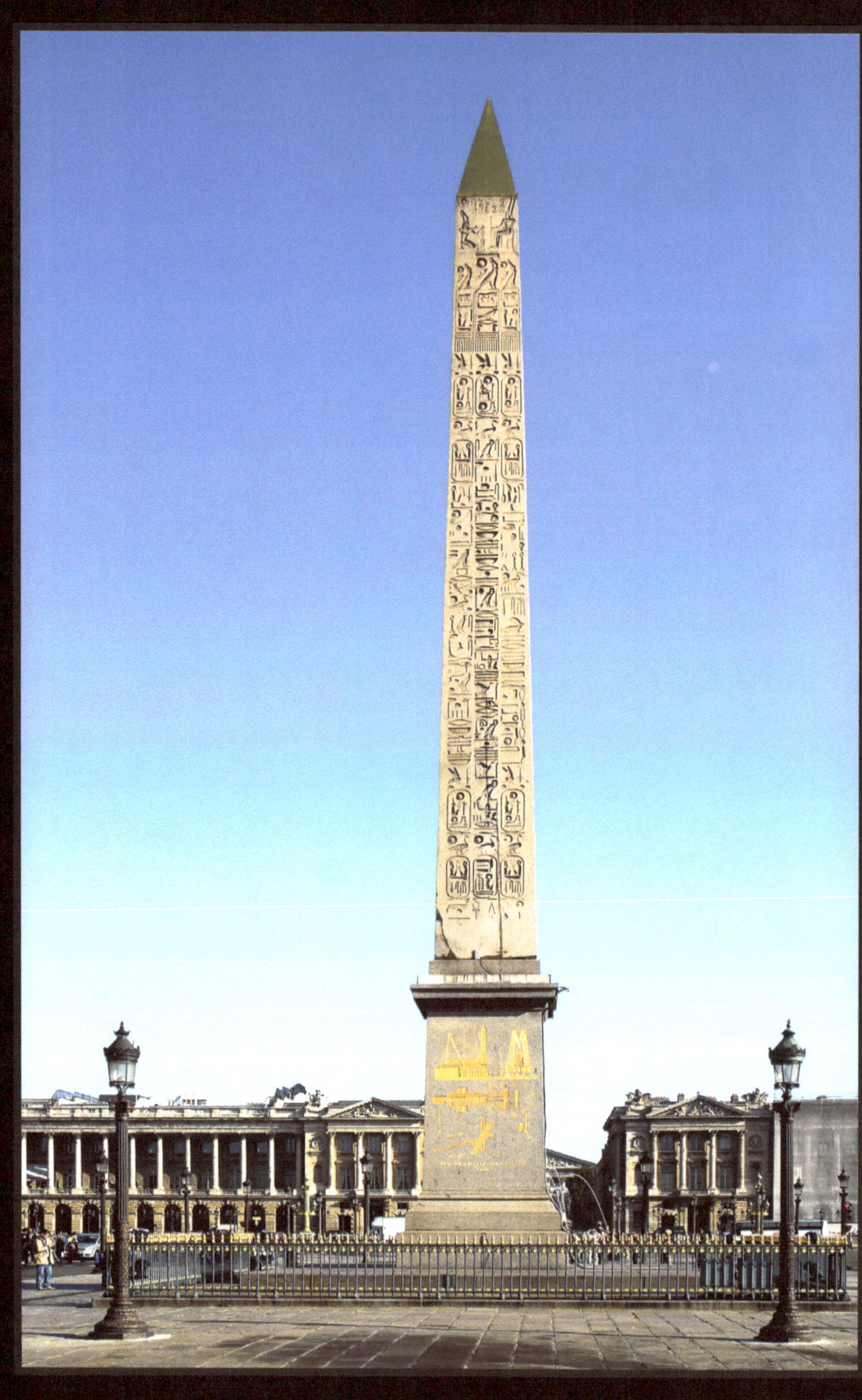

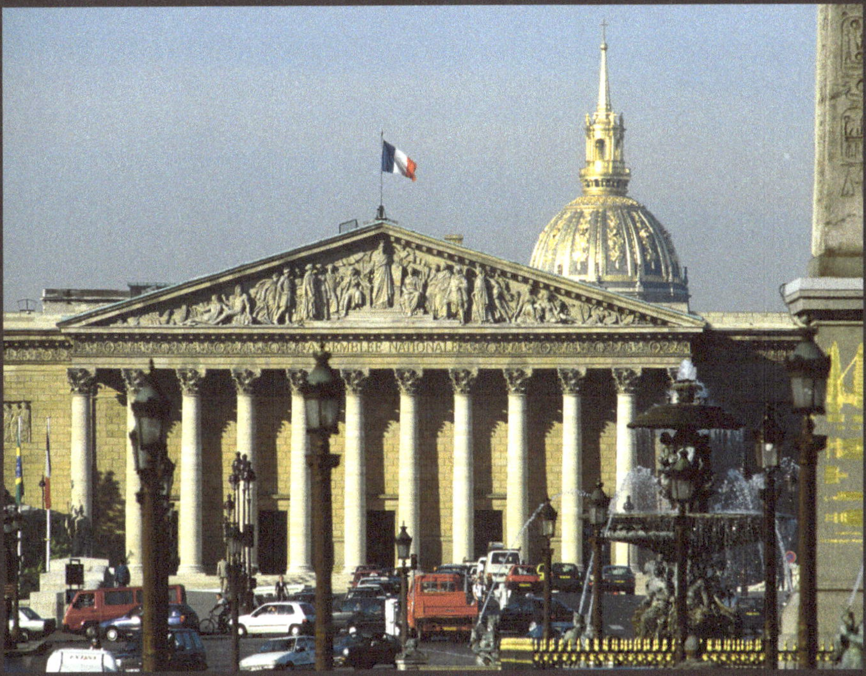

The Concorde Square

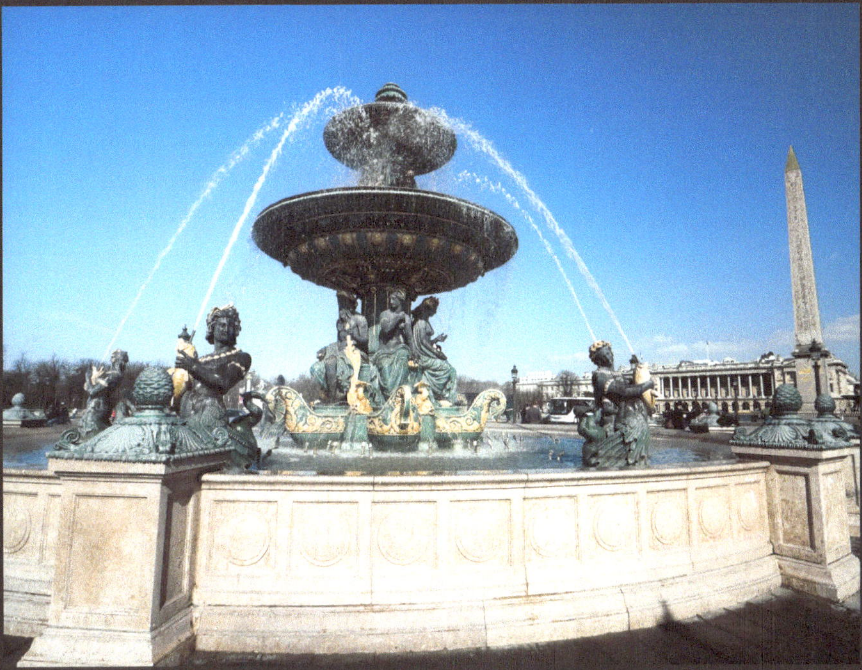

Luxembourg Gardens

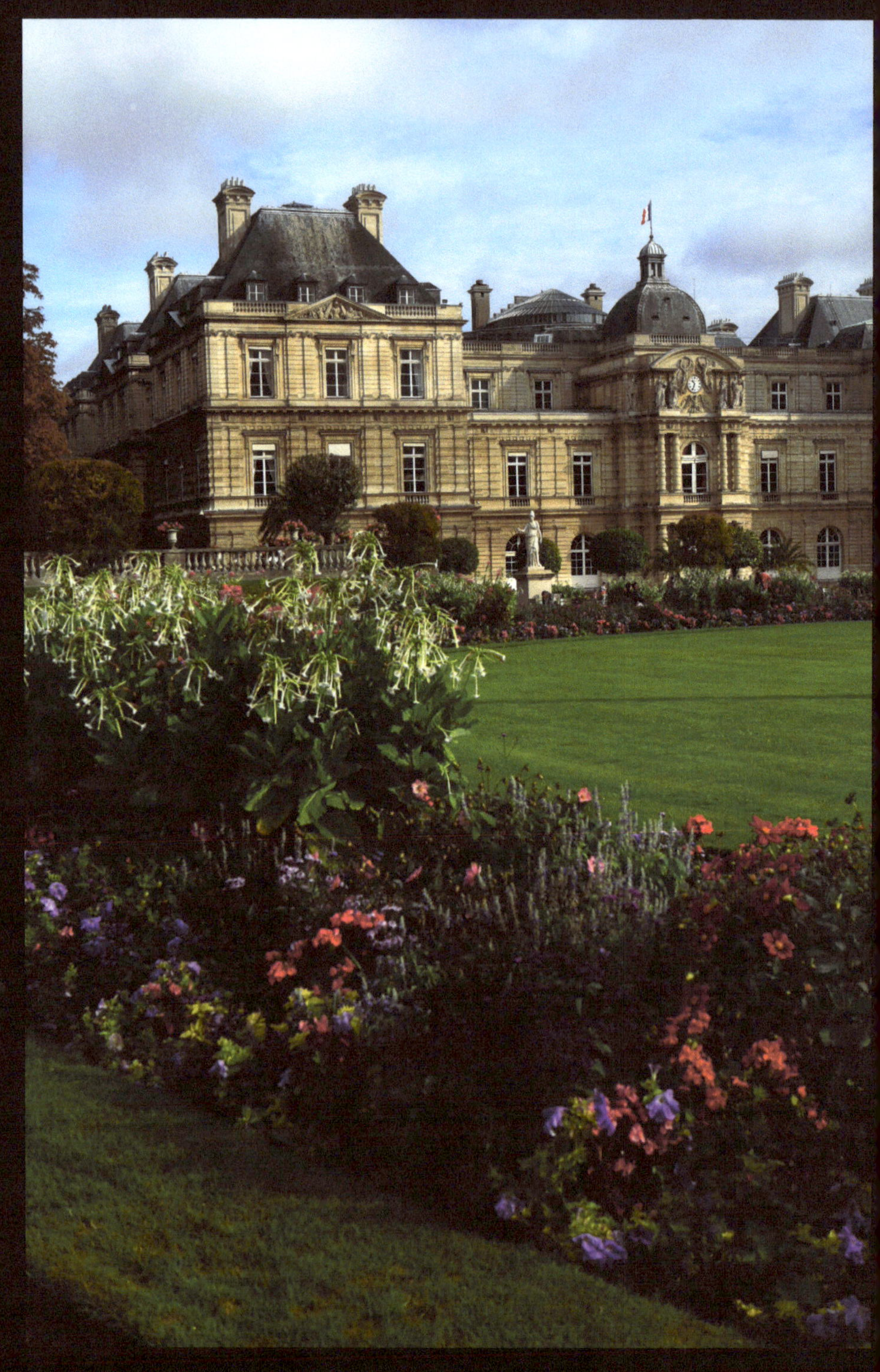

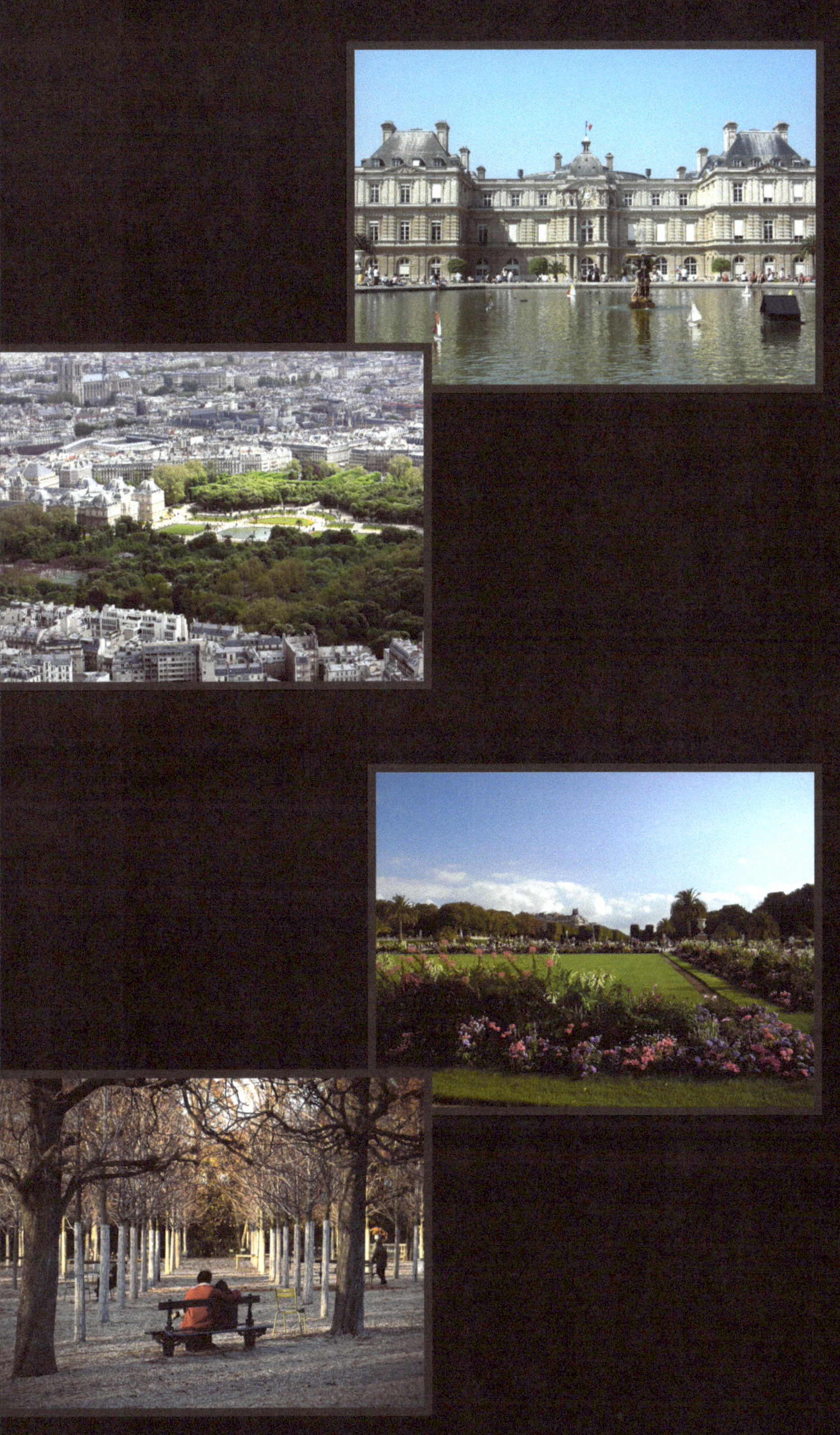

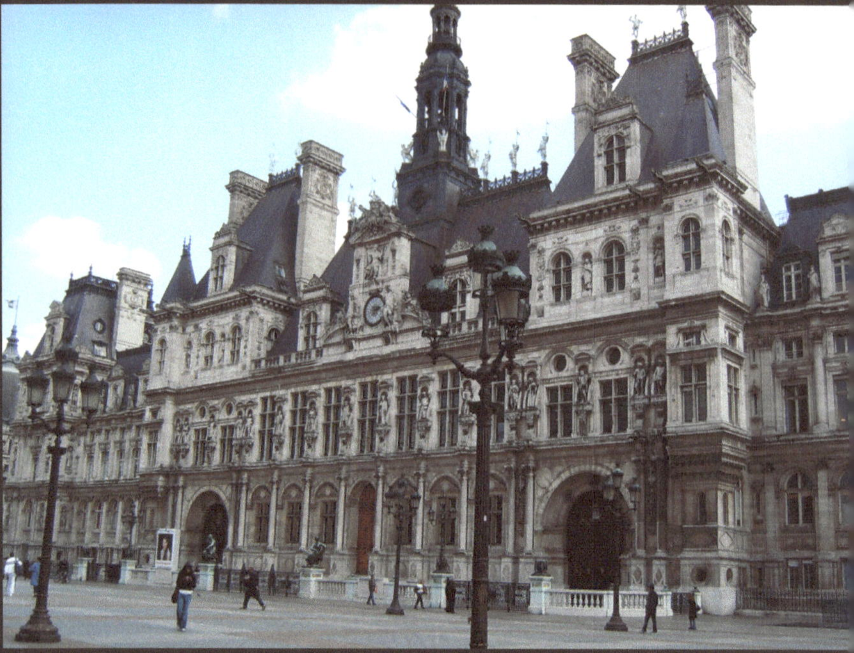

City Hall

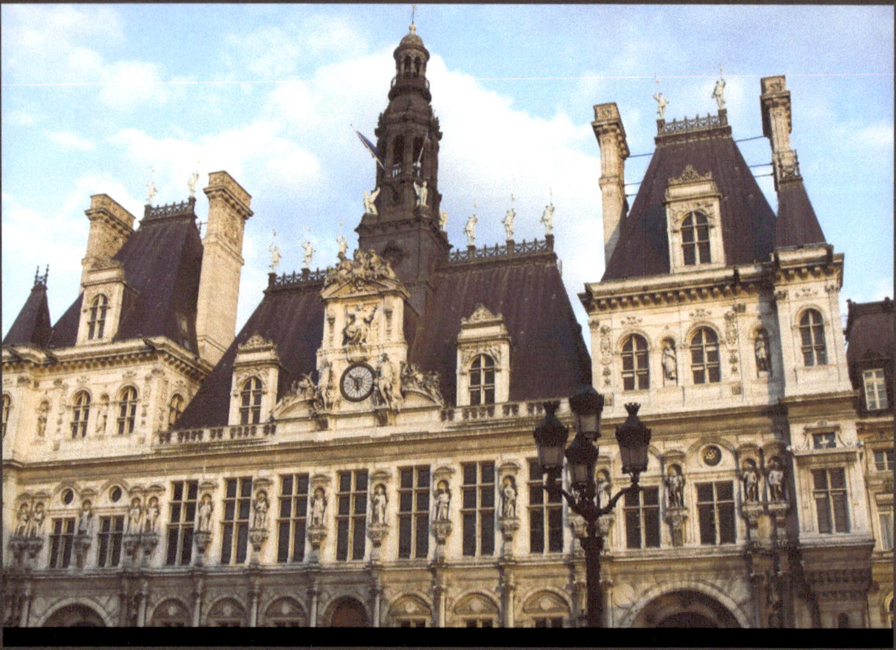

Saint - Jacques Tower

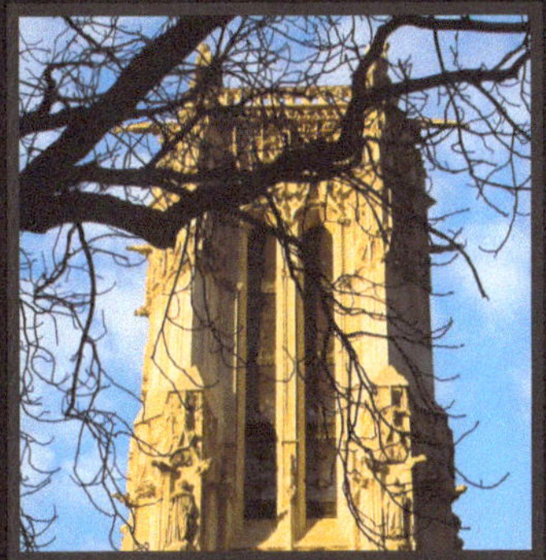

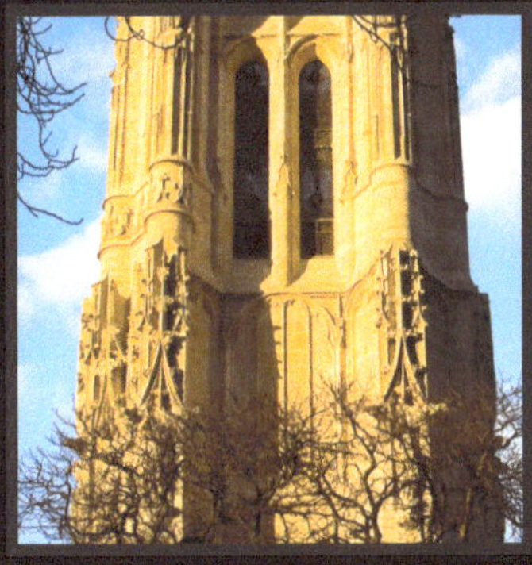

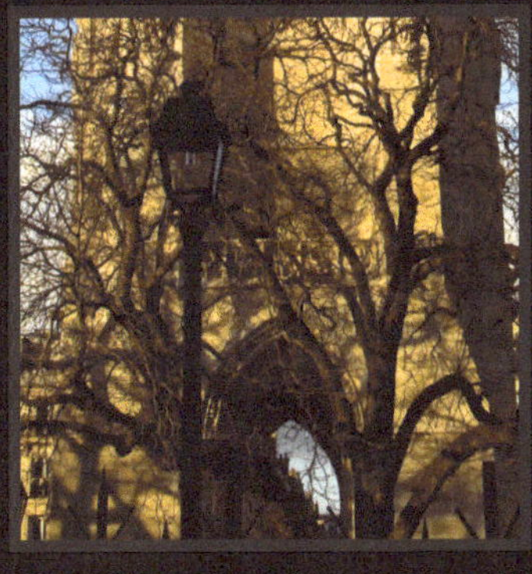

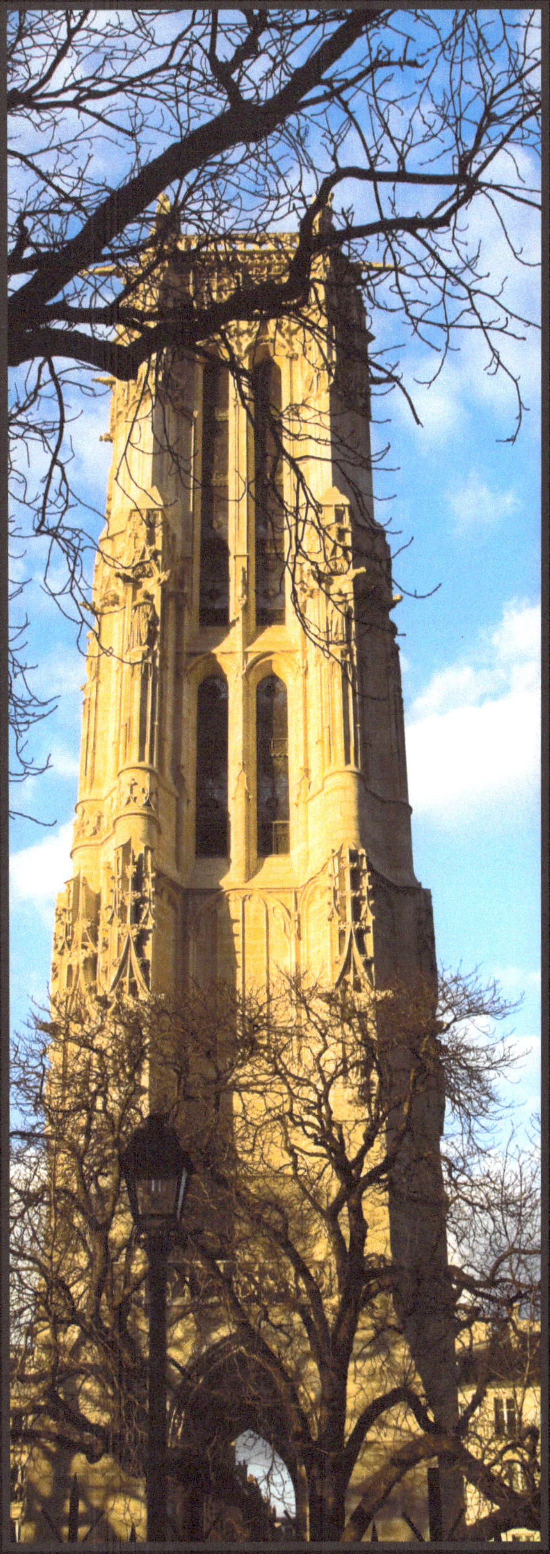

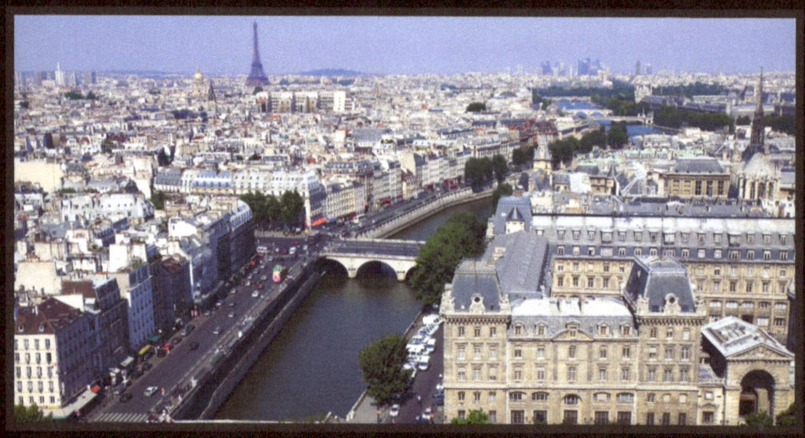

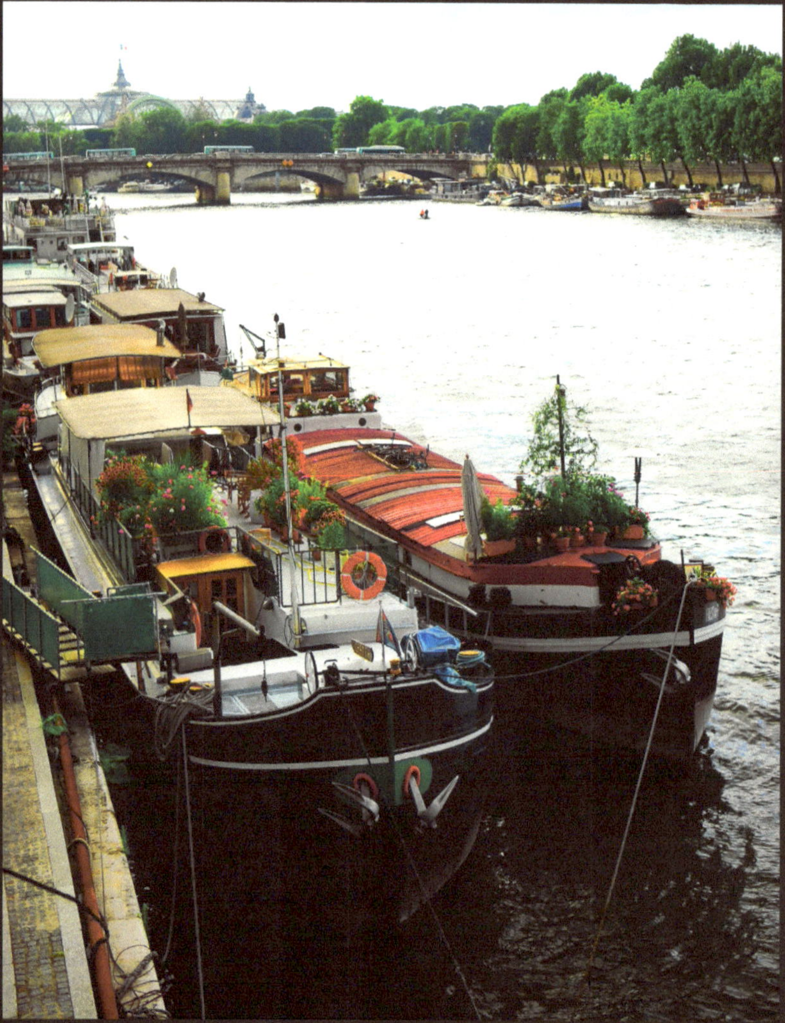

The Seine River

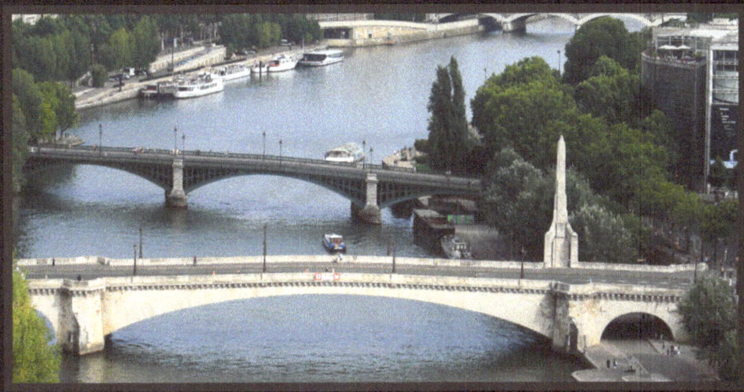

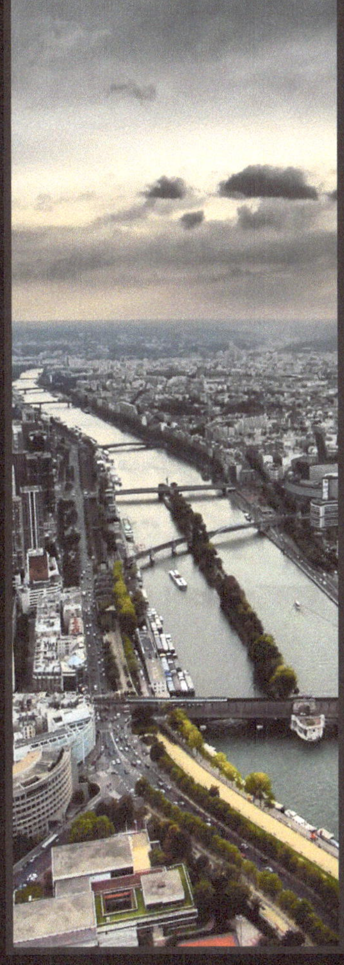

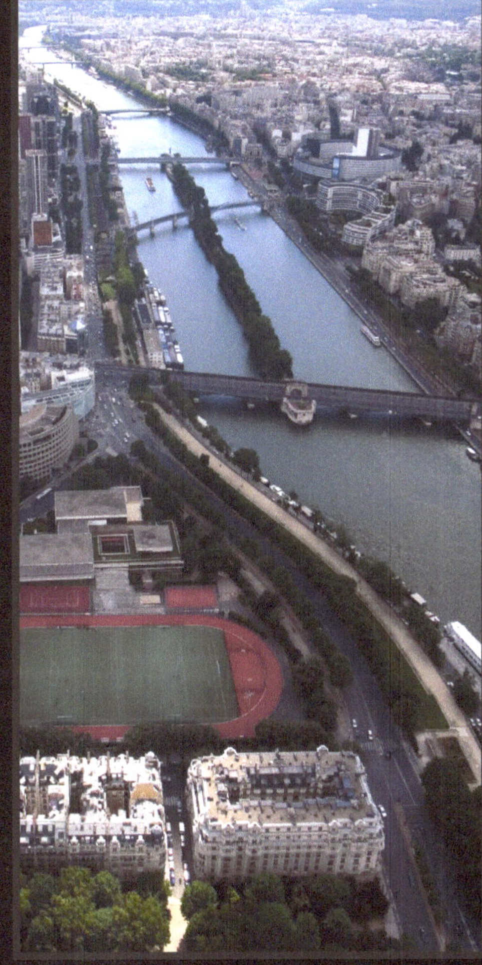

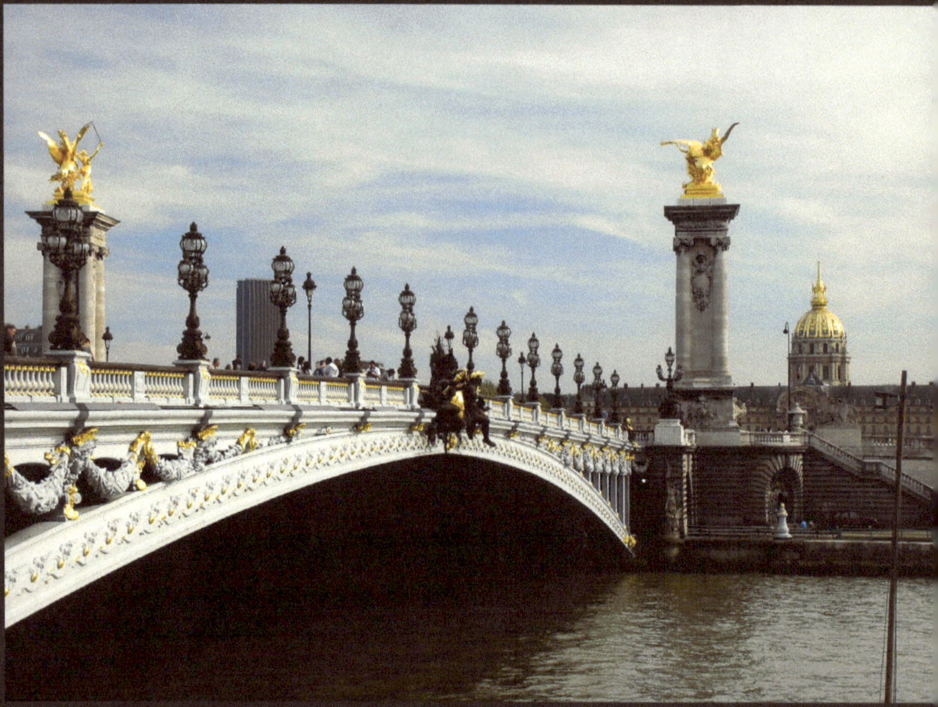

The Seine River Bridges

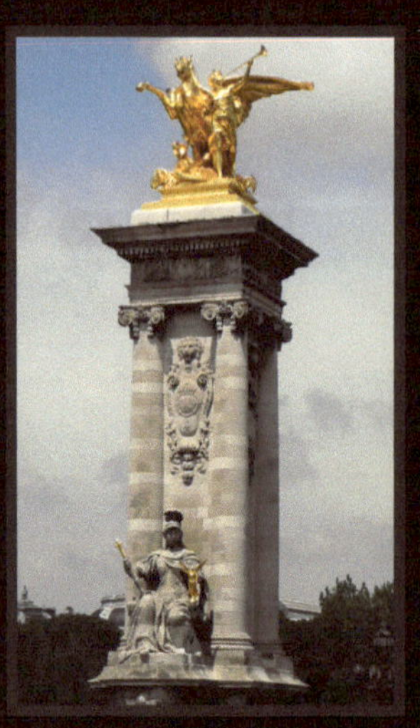

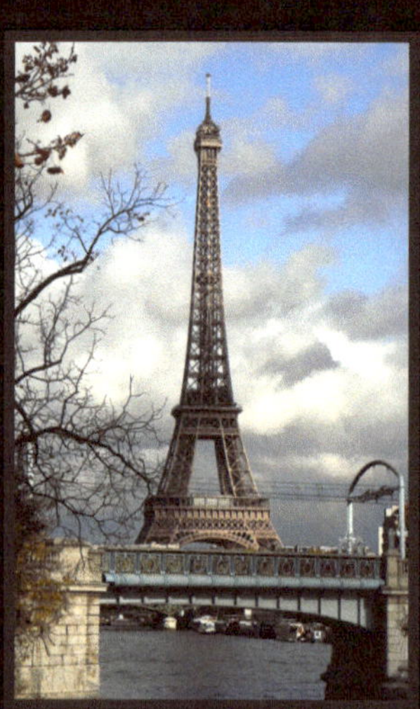

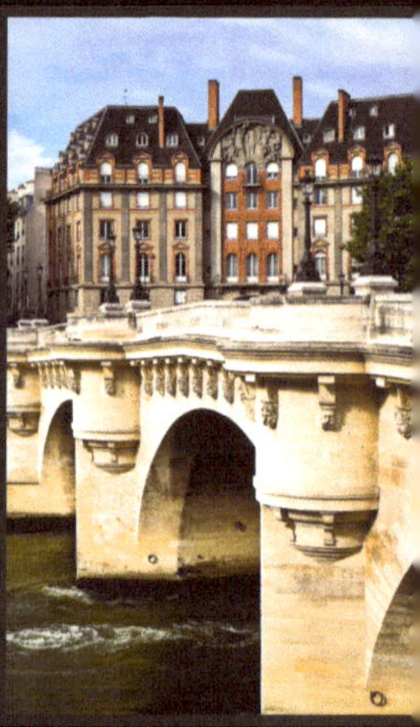

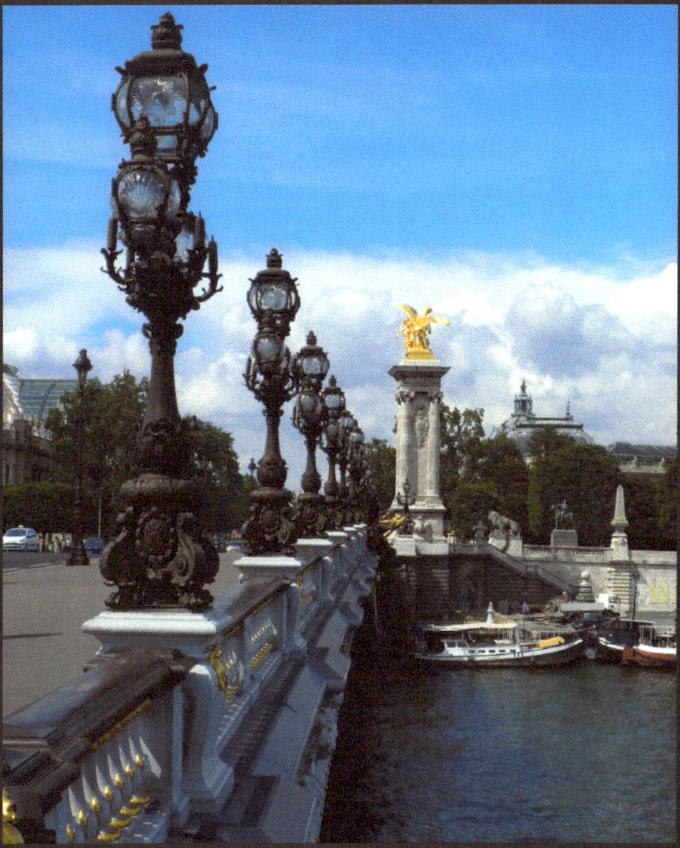

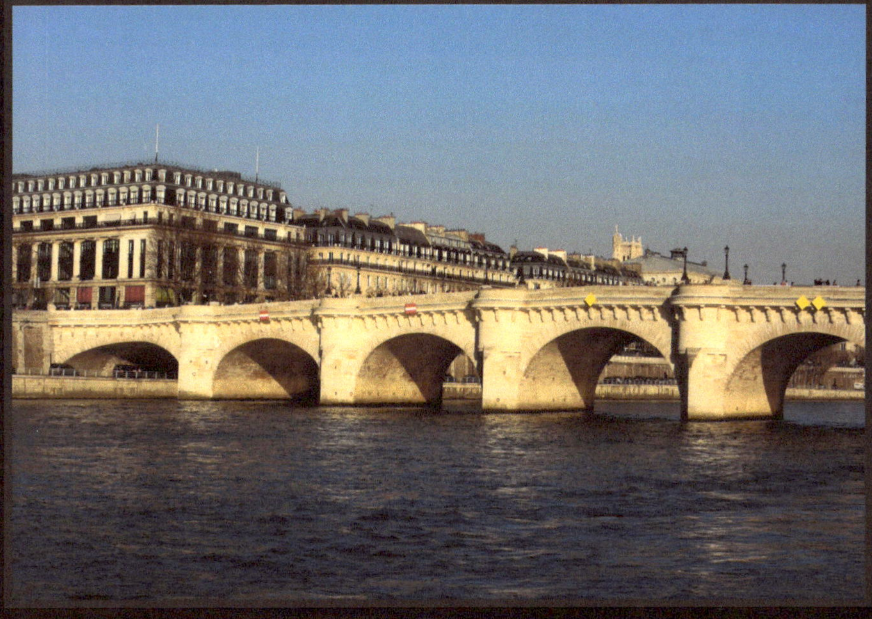

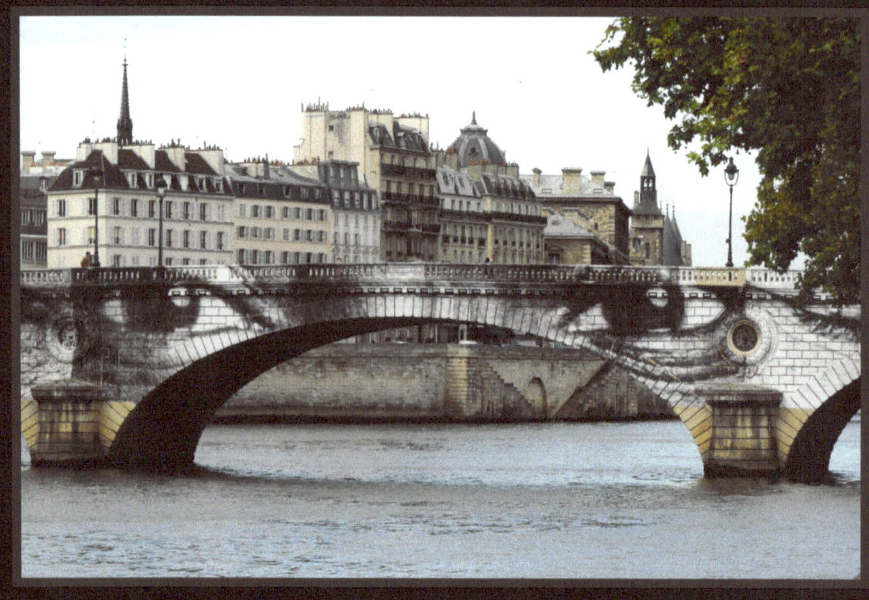

EYES ON PARIS

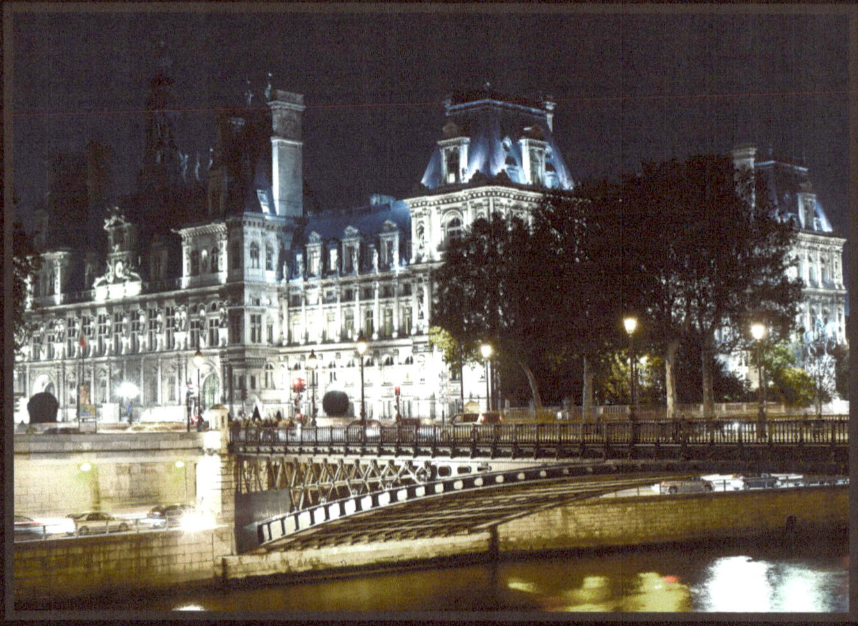

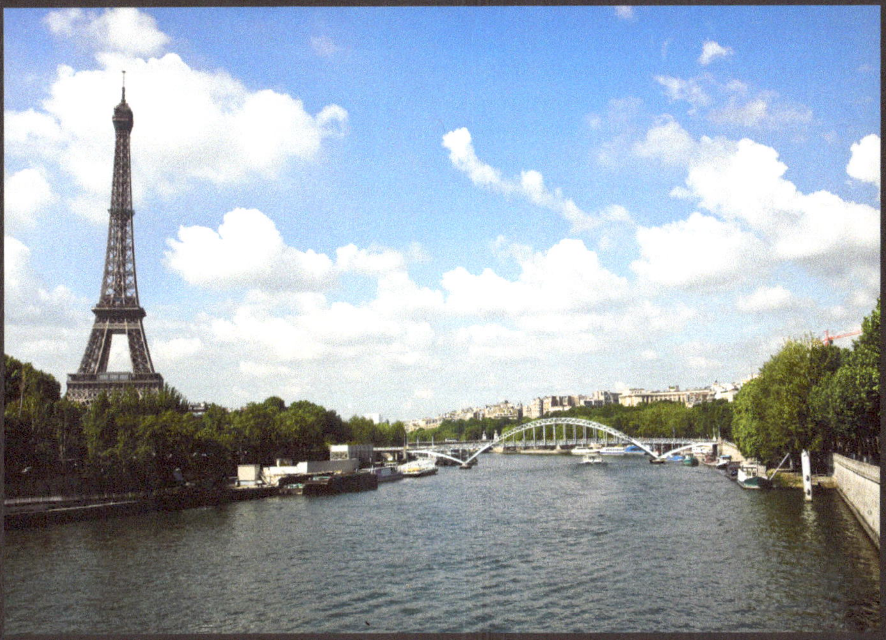

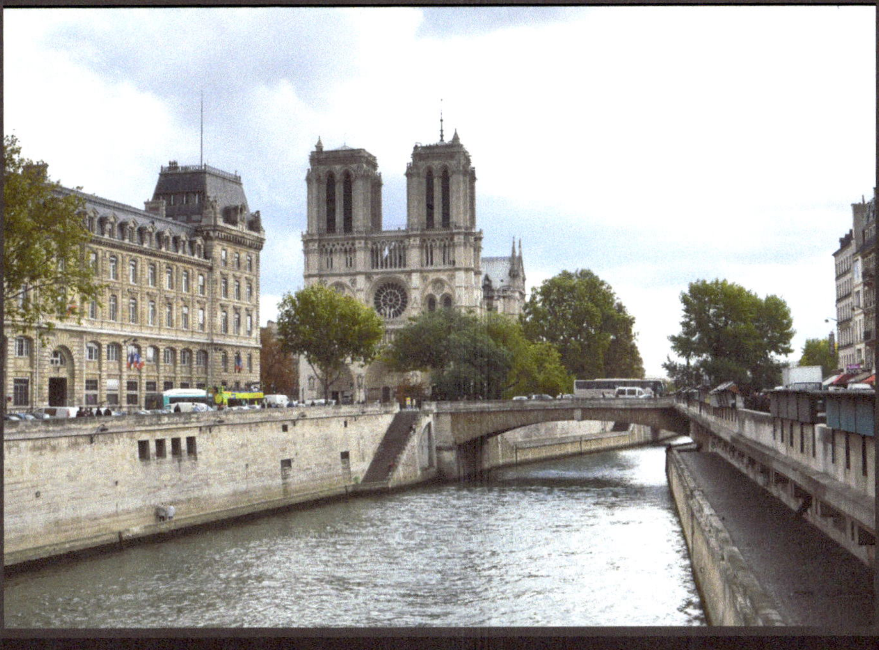

Champs - Elysées

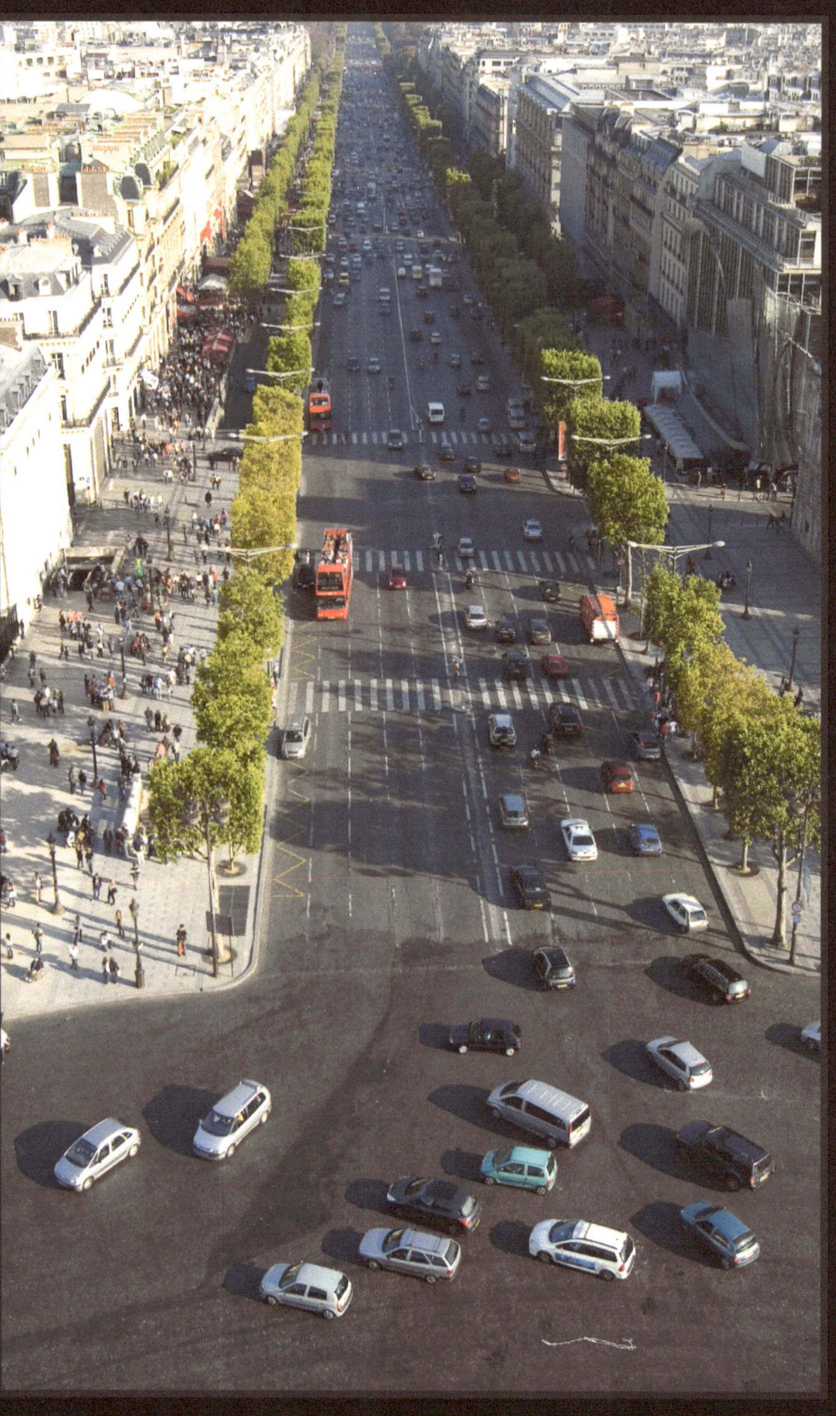

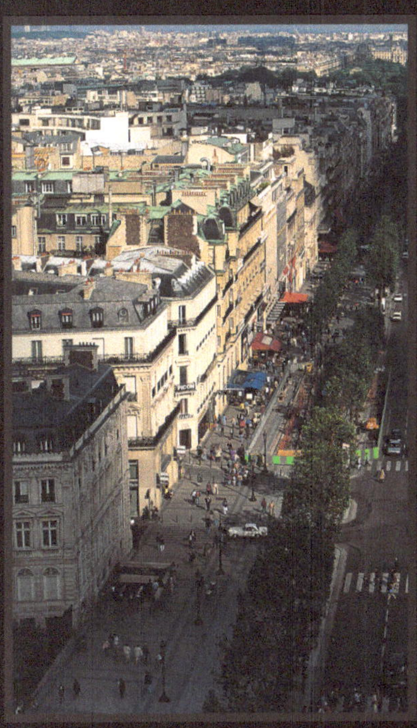

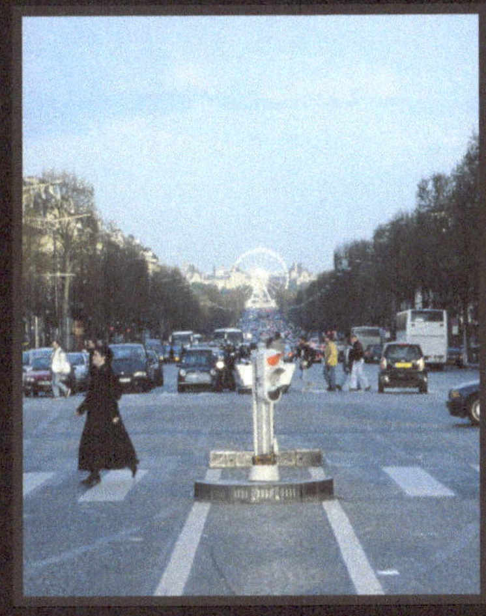

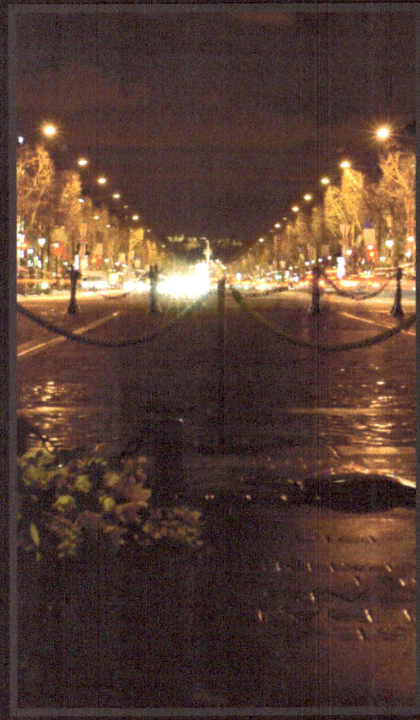

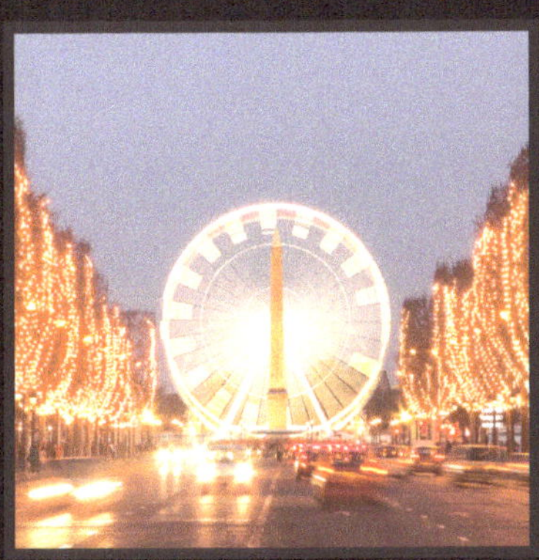

La Défense

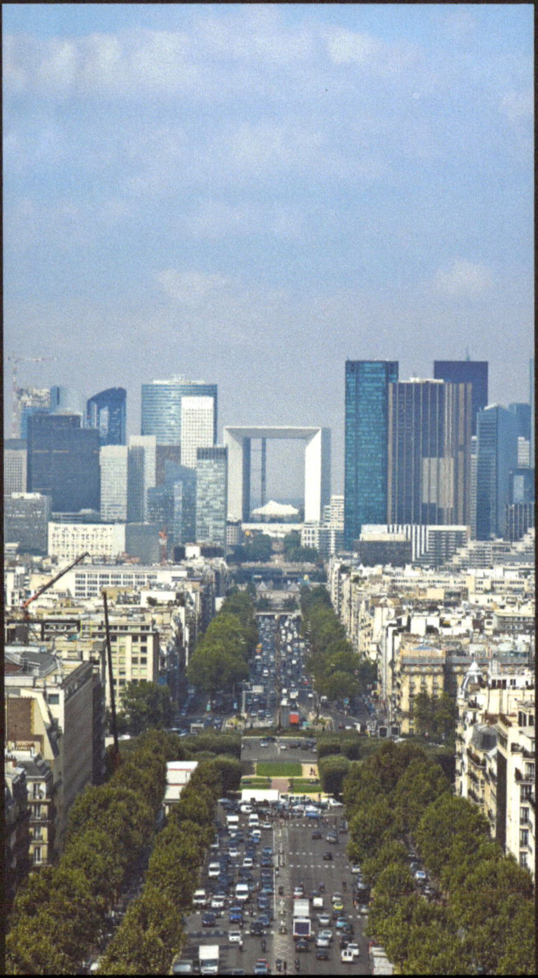

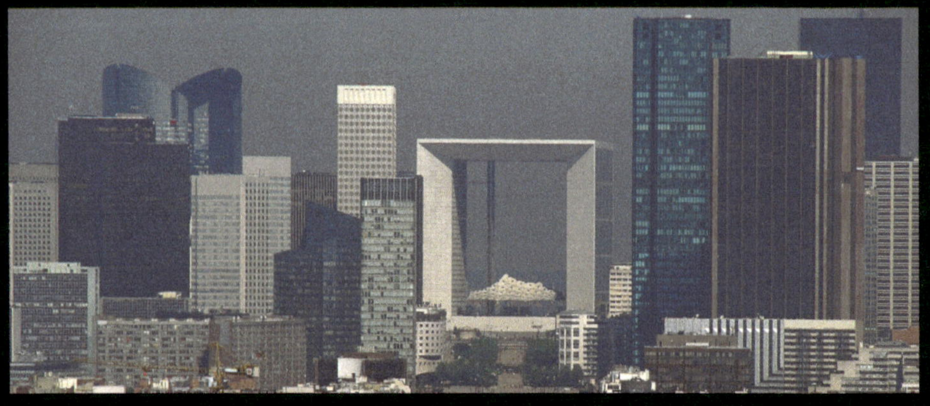

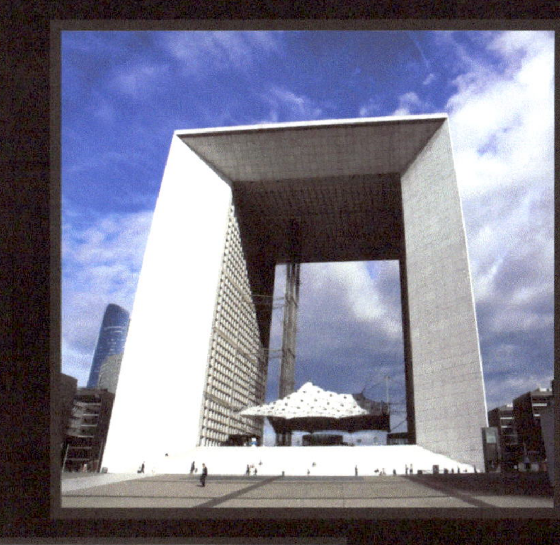

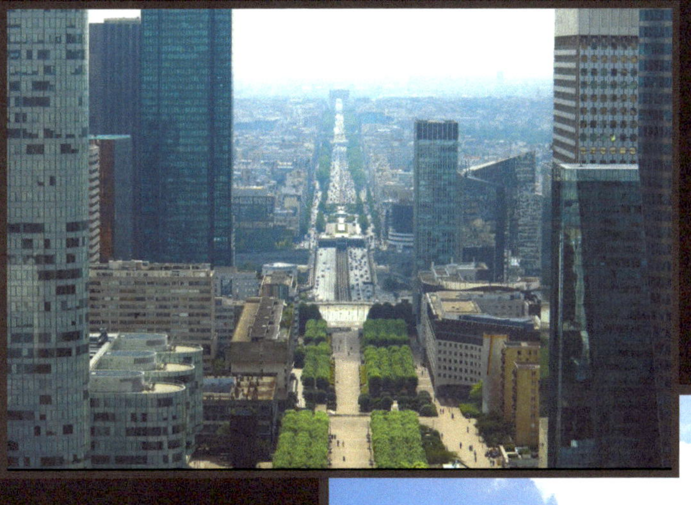

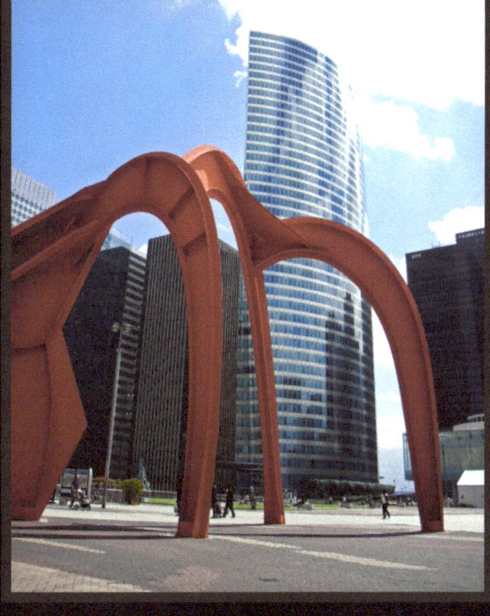

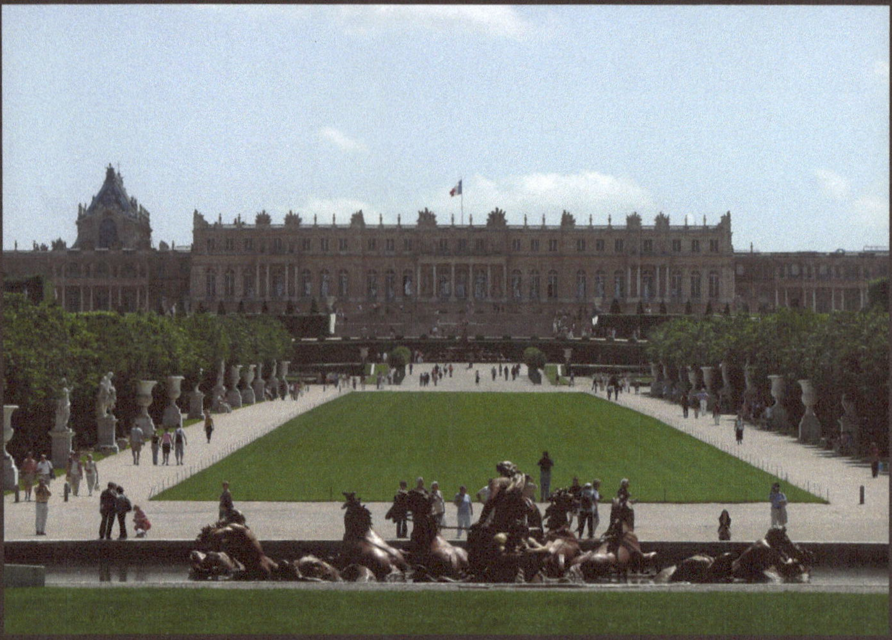

PALACE OF VERSAILLES

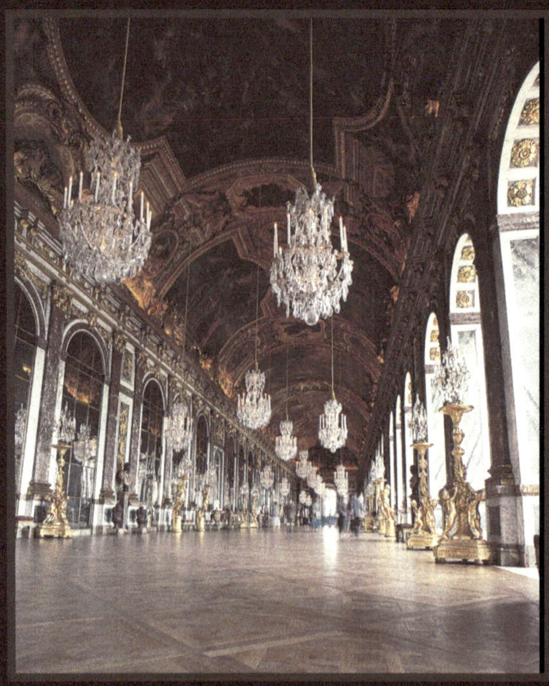

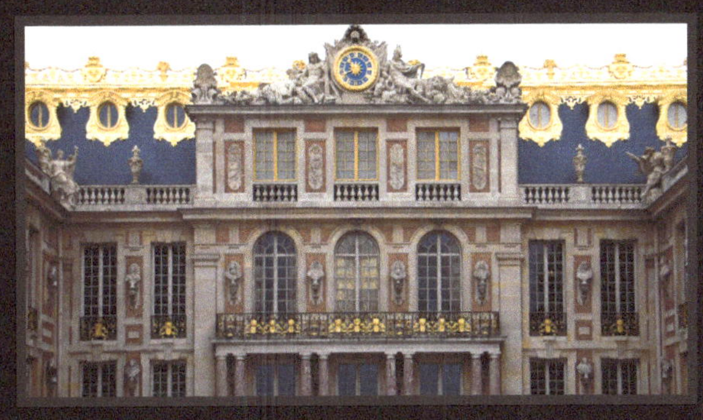

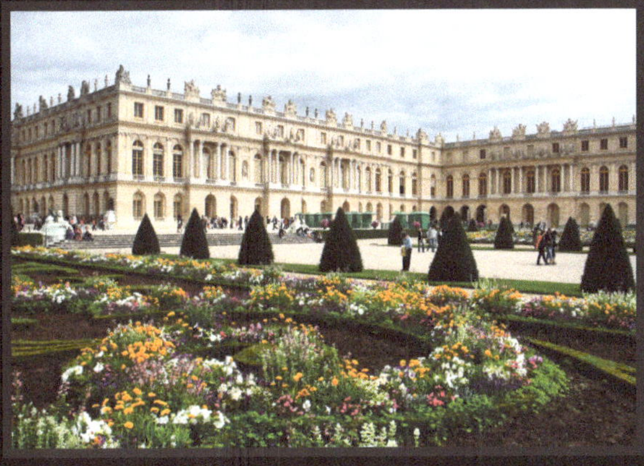

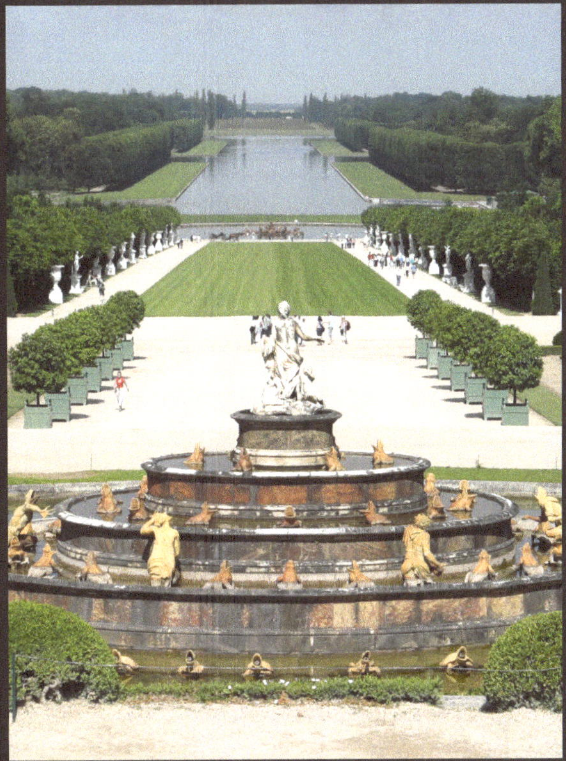

Rodin Museum

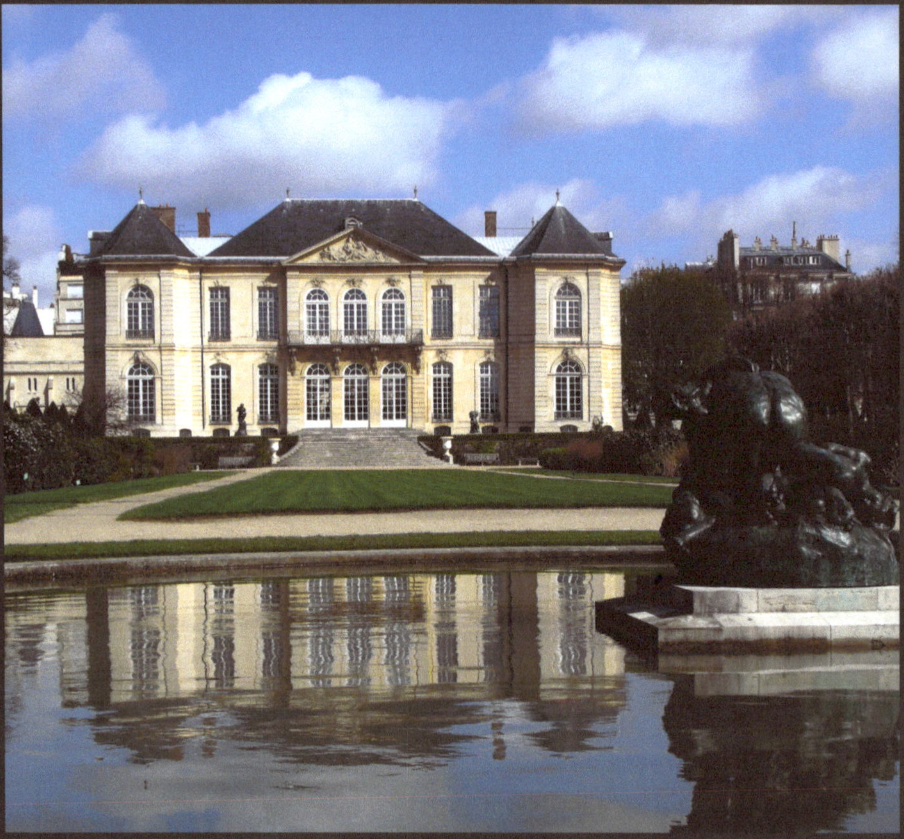

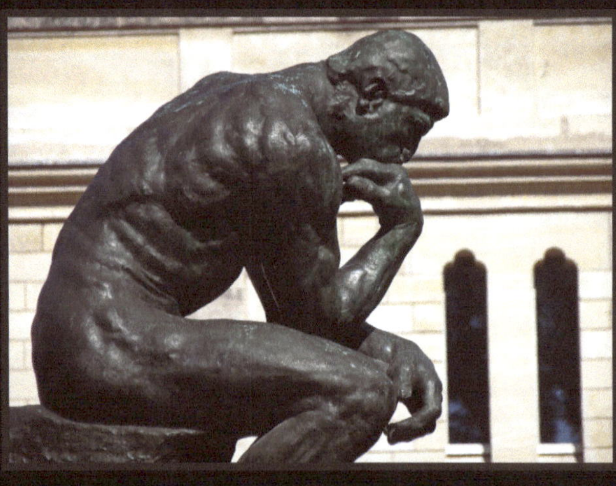

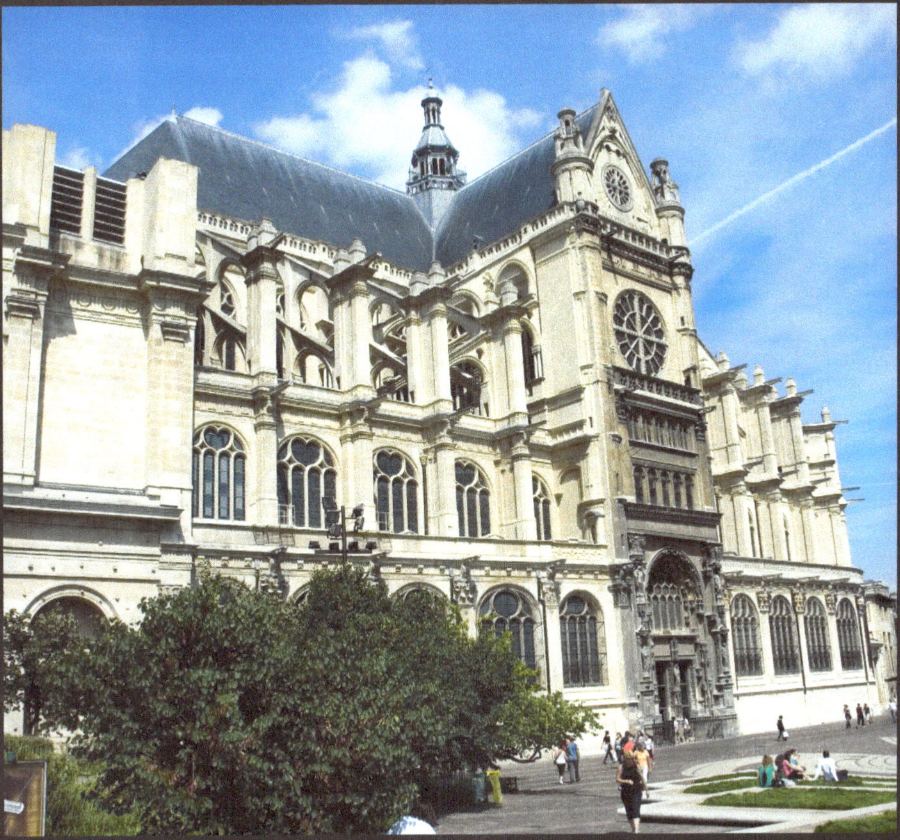

Forum des Halles

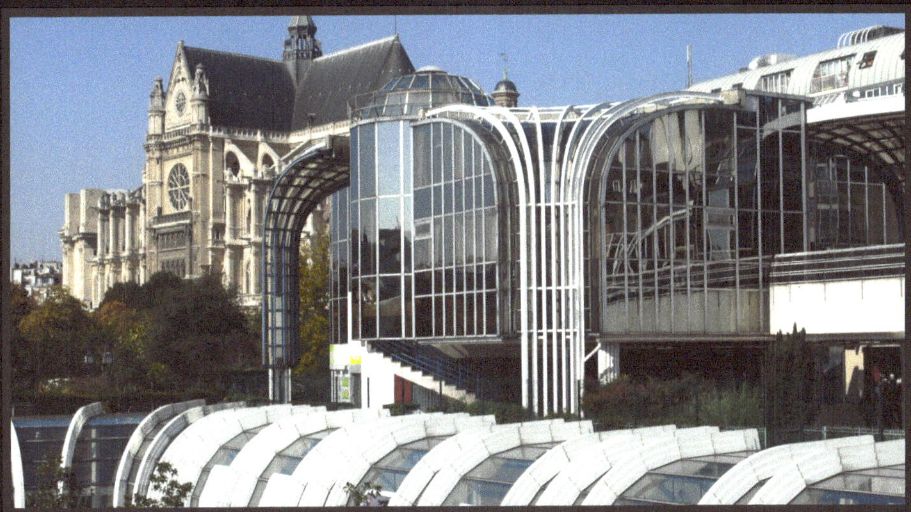

La Conciergerie

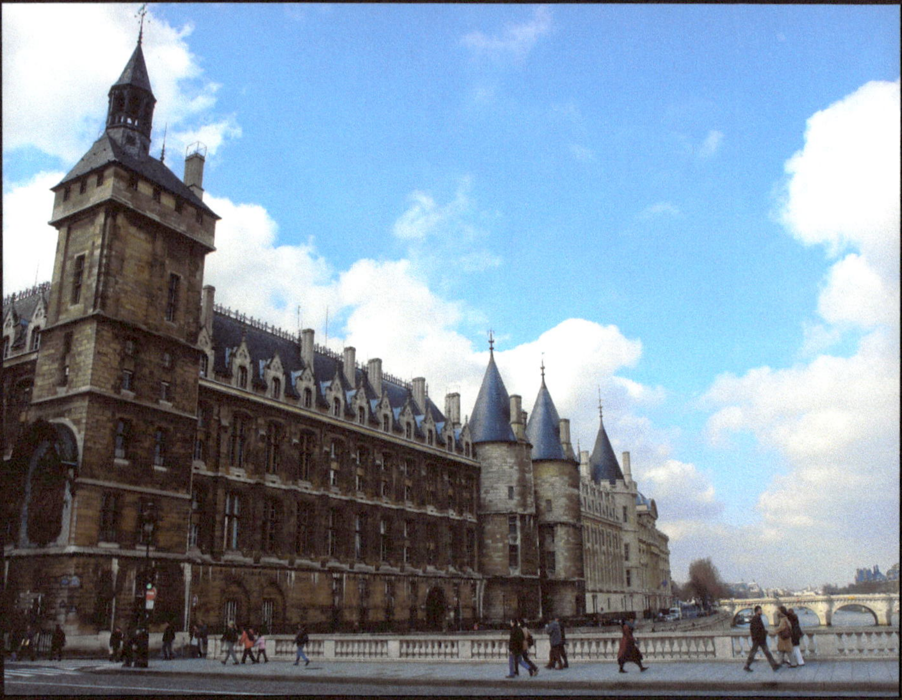

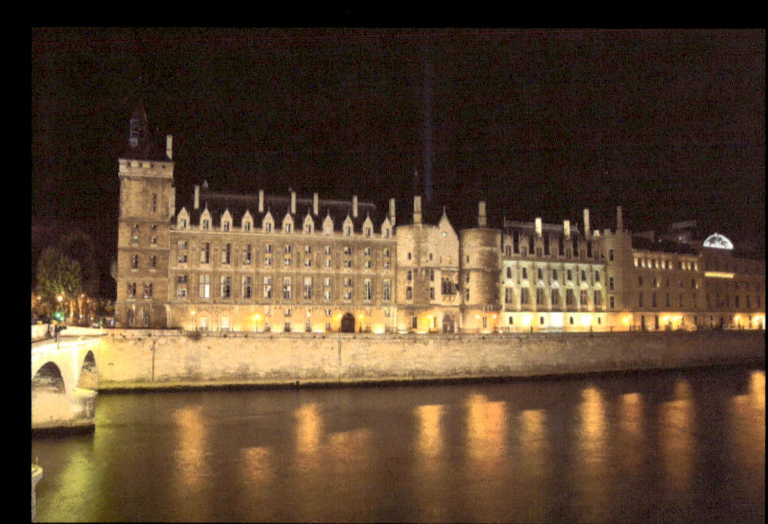

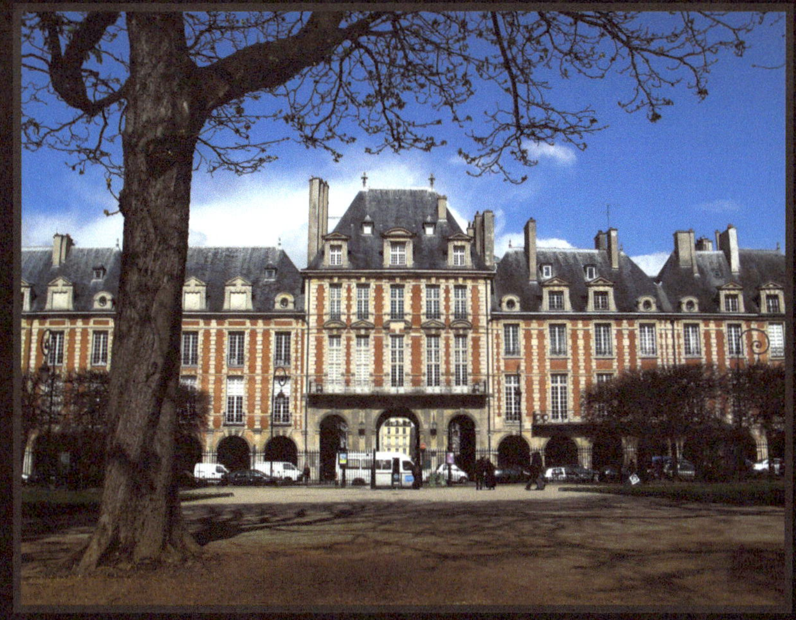

THE VOSGES SQUARE

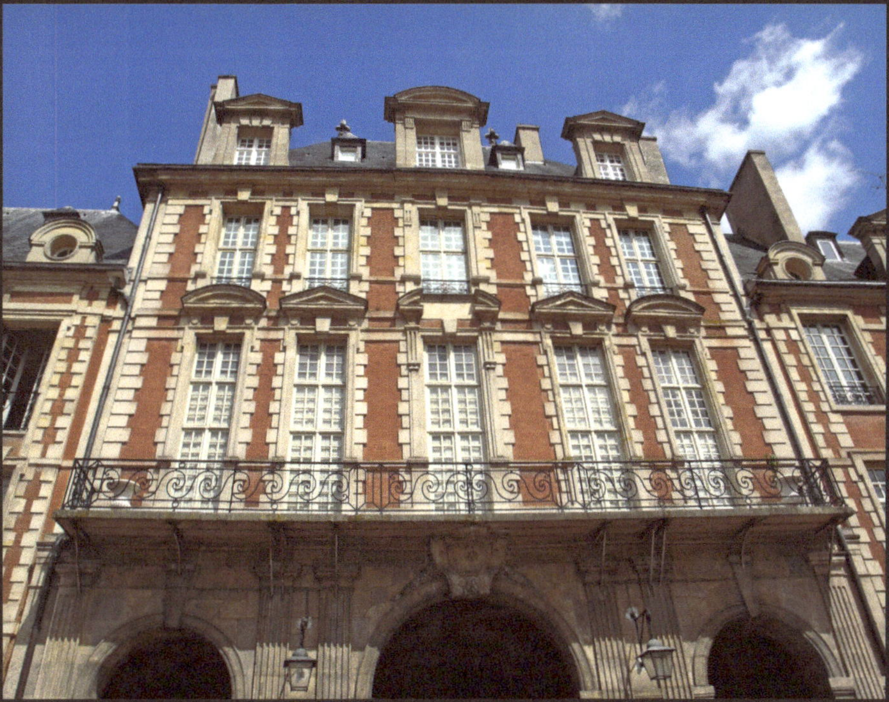

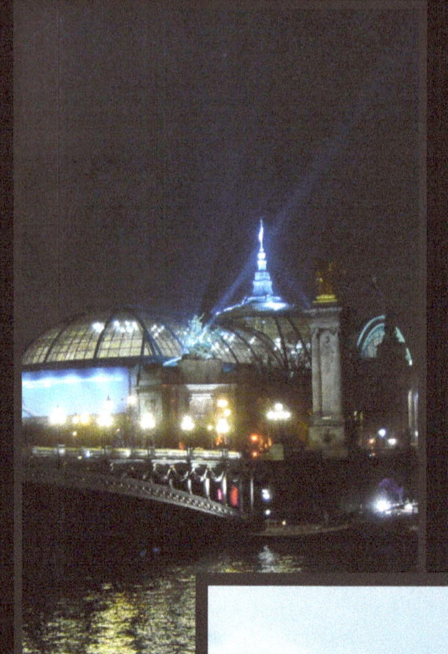

GRAND PALAIS

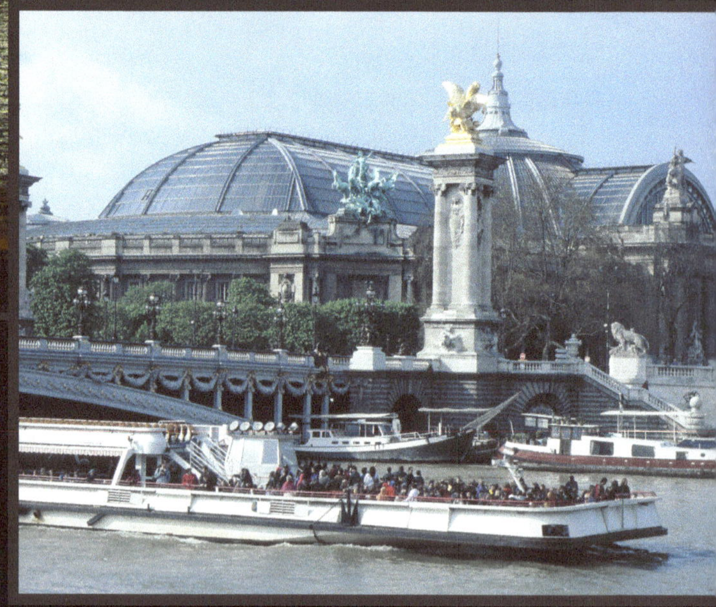

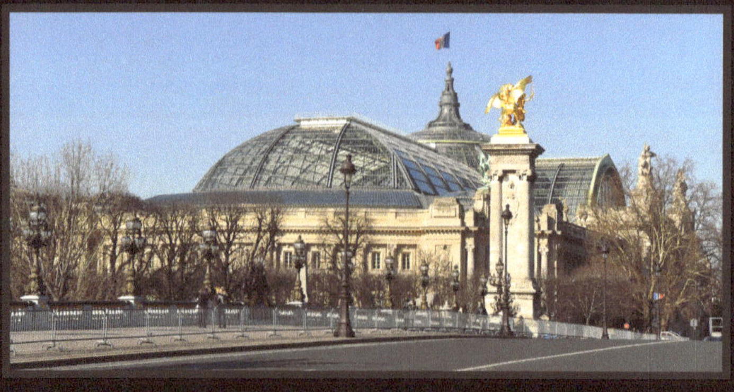

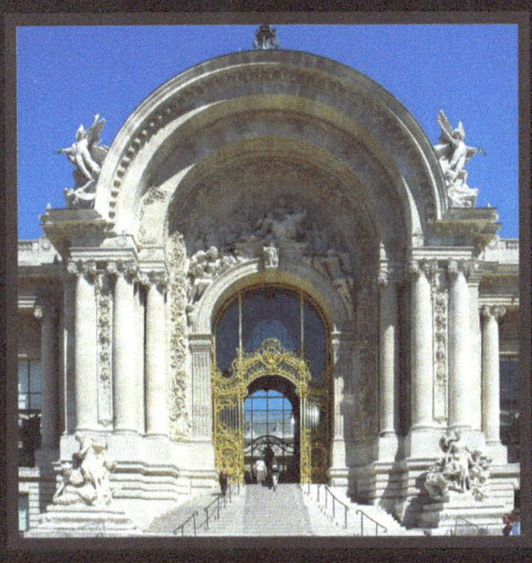

Petit Palais

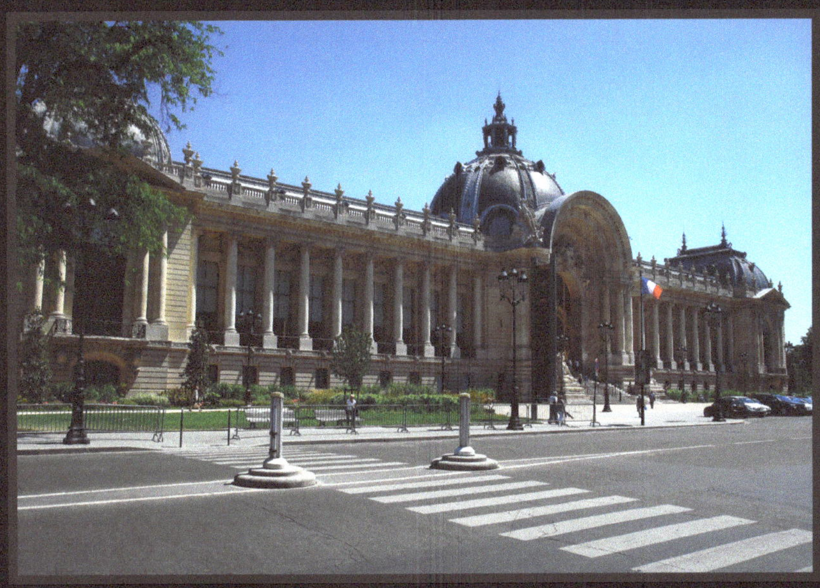

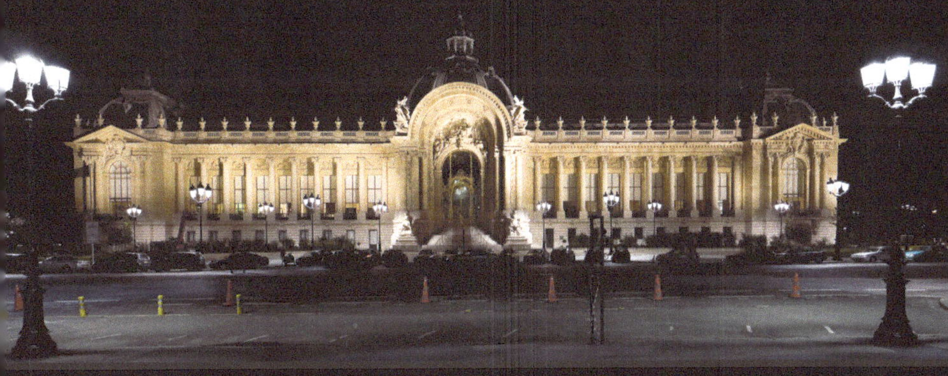

Champs de Mars

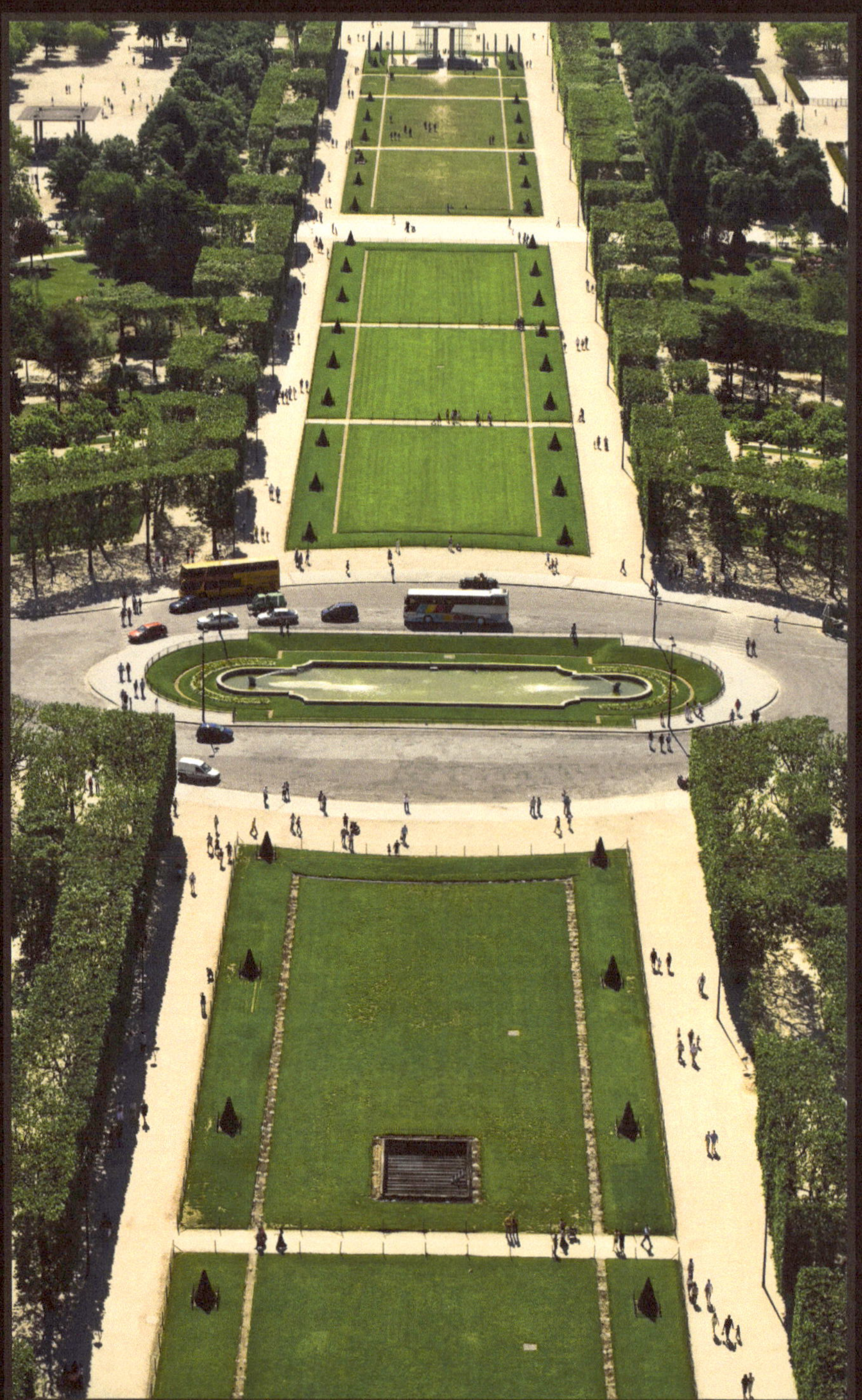

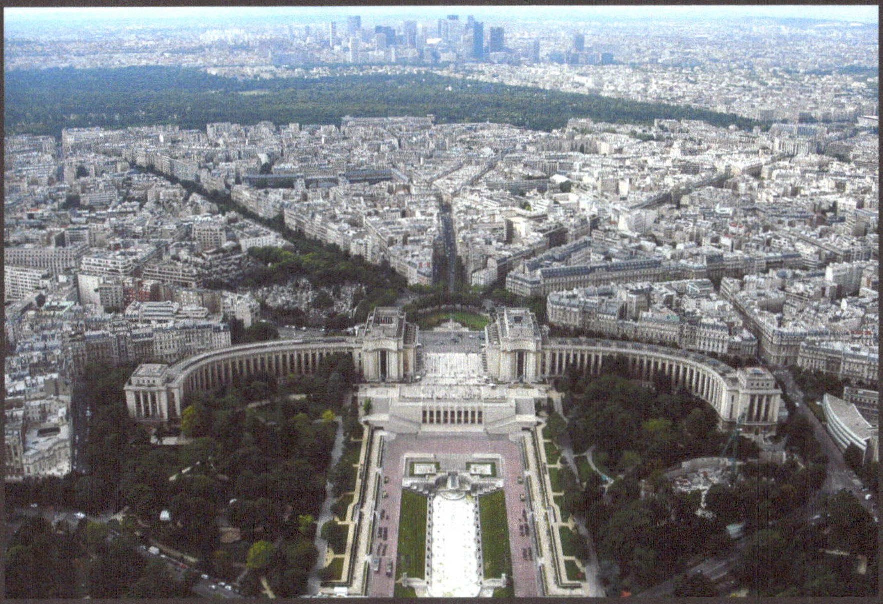

The Trocadero

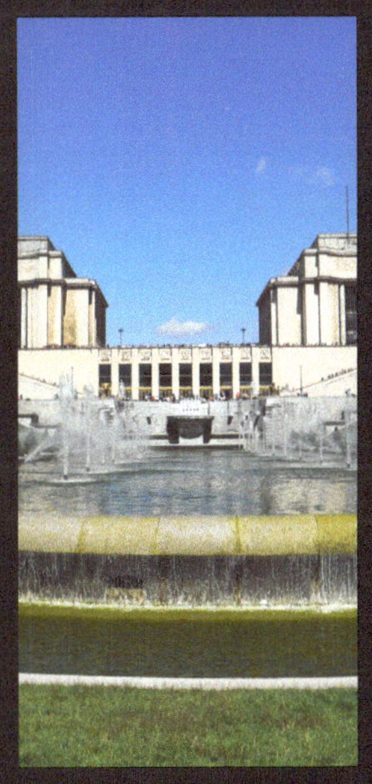

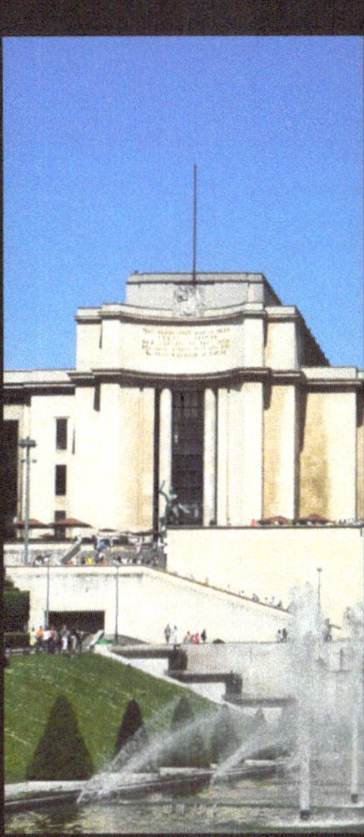

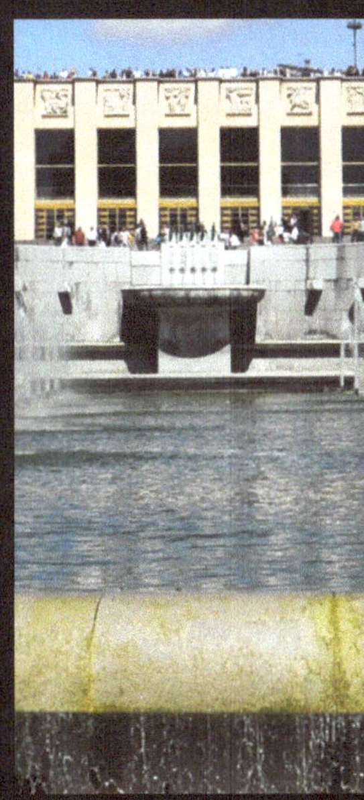

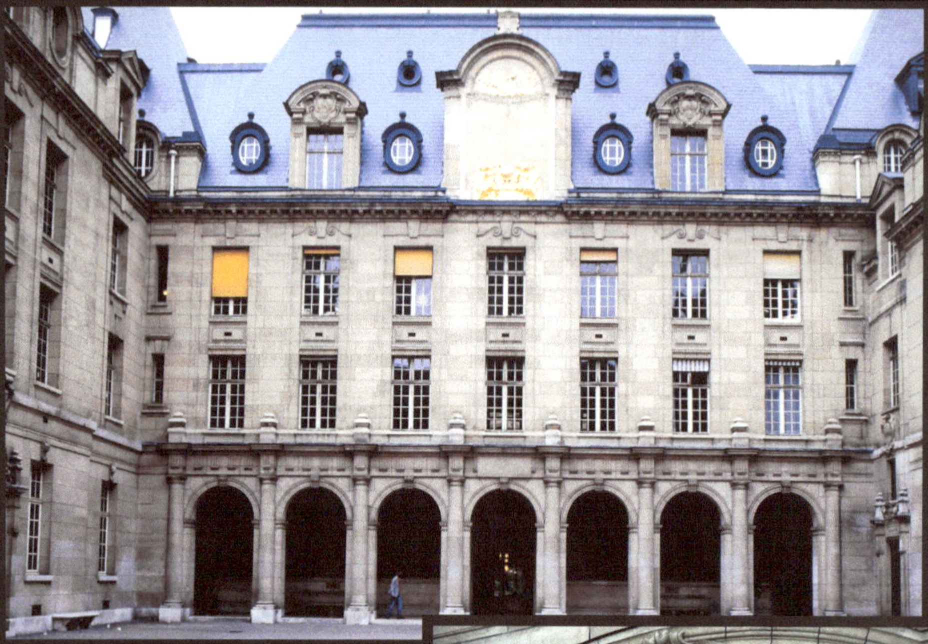

Sorbonne University

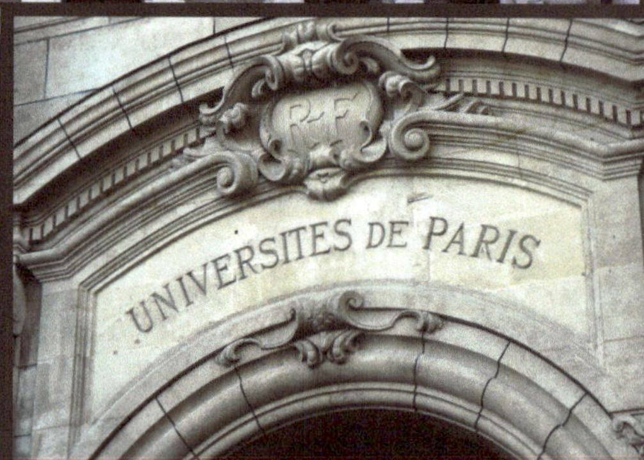

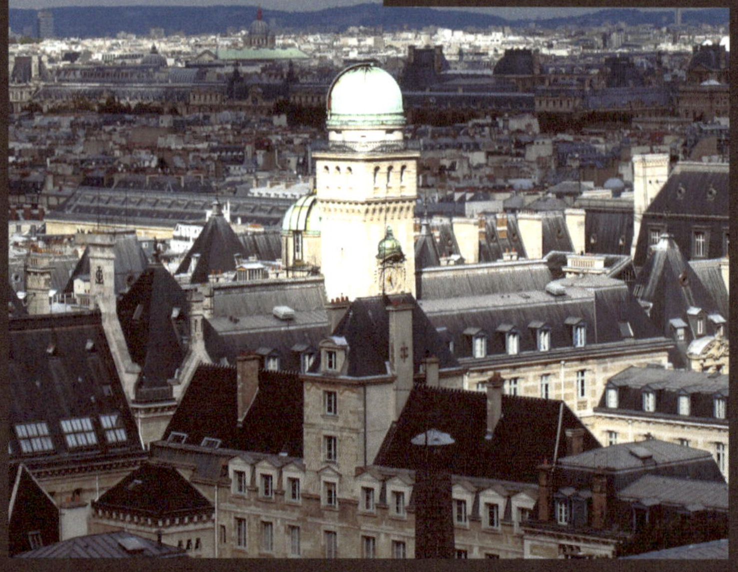

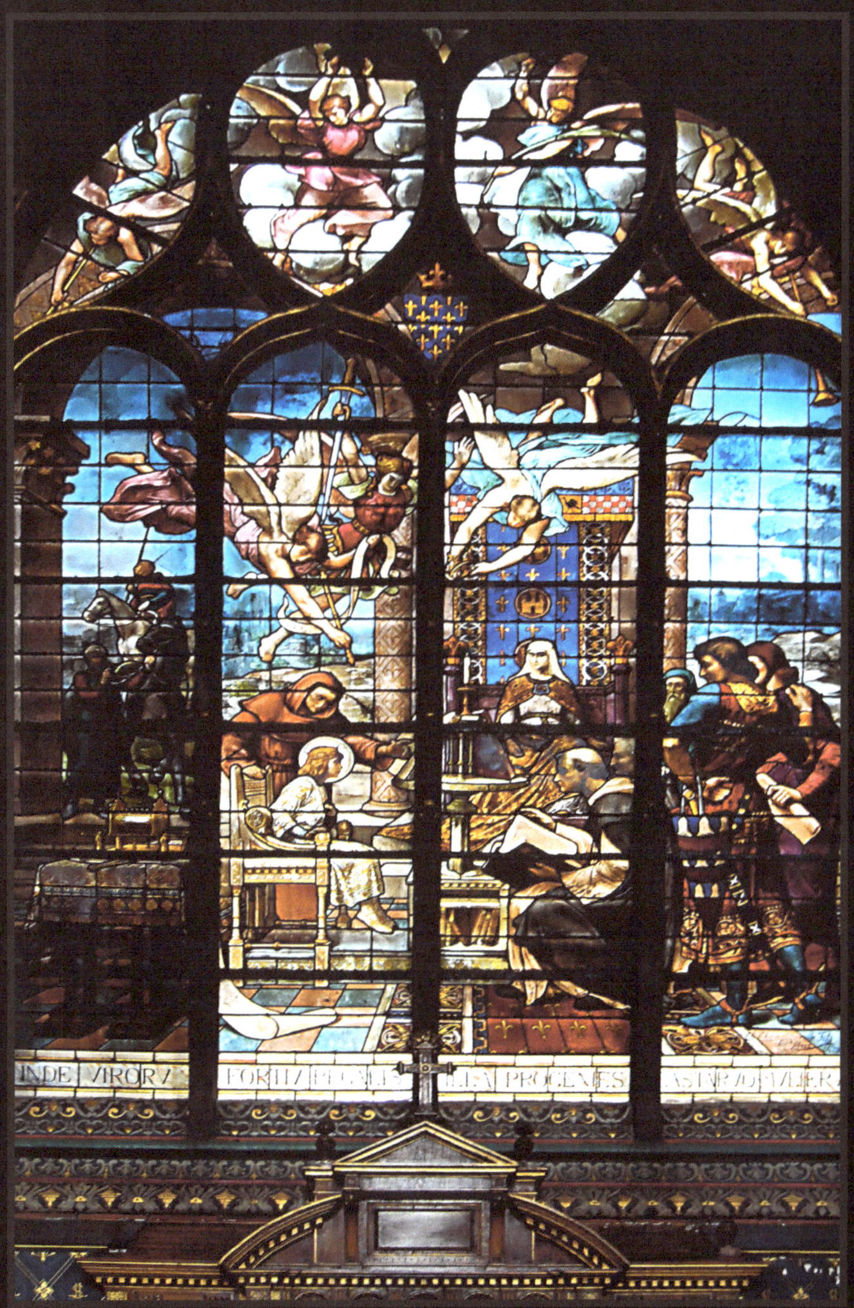

STAINED - GLASS
WINDOW IN CHURCH

La Bastille Square

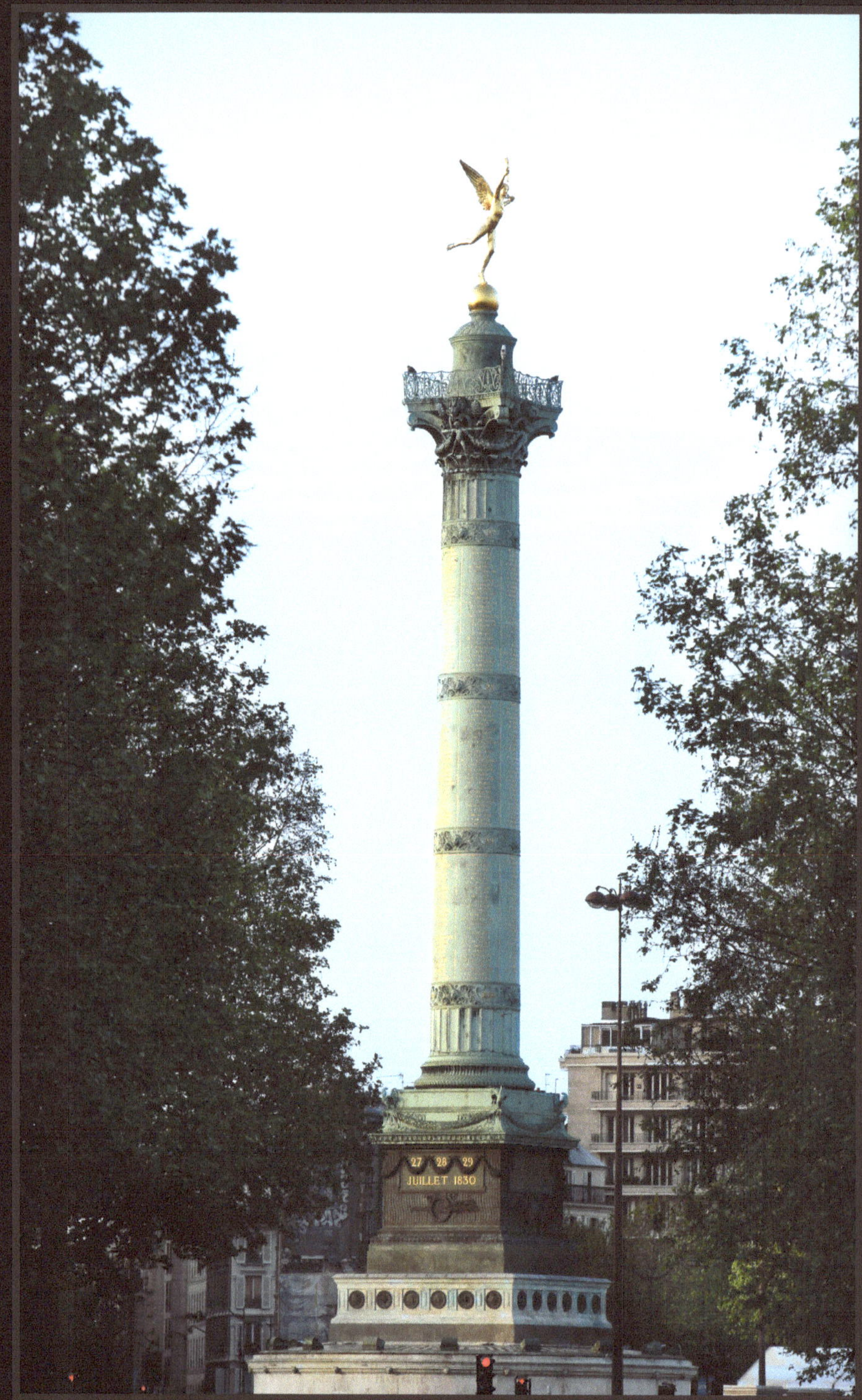

The Medicis Fountain

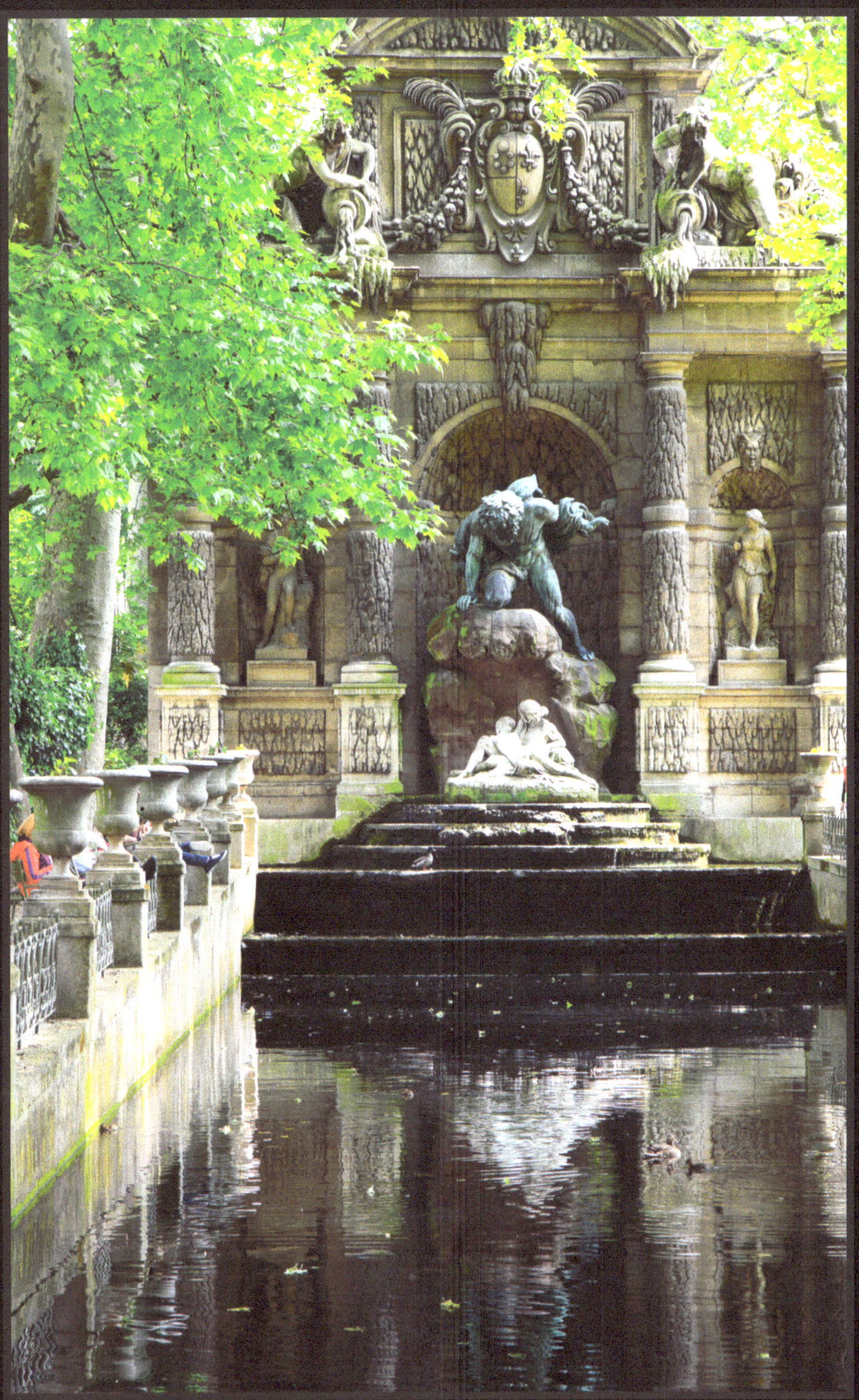

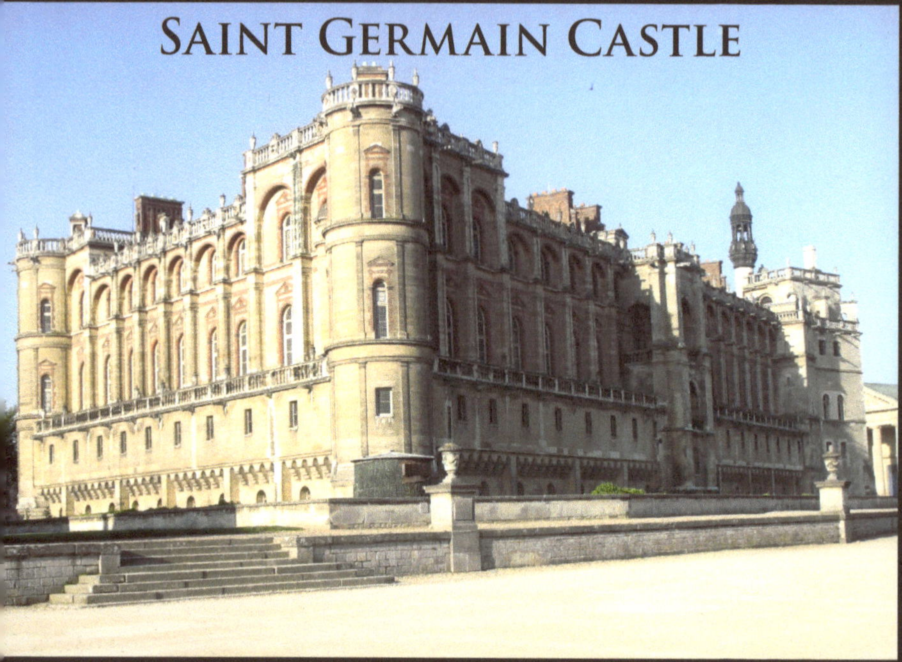

Saint Germain Castle

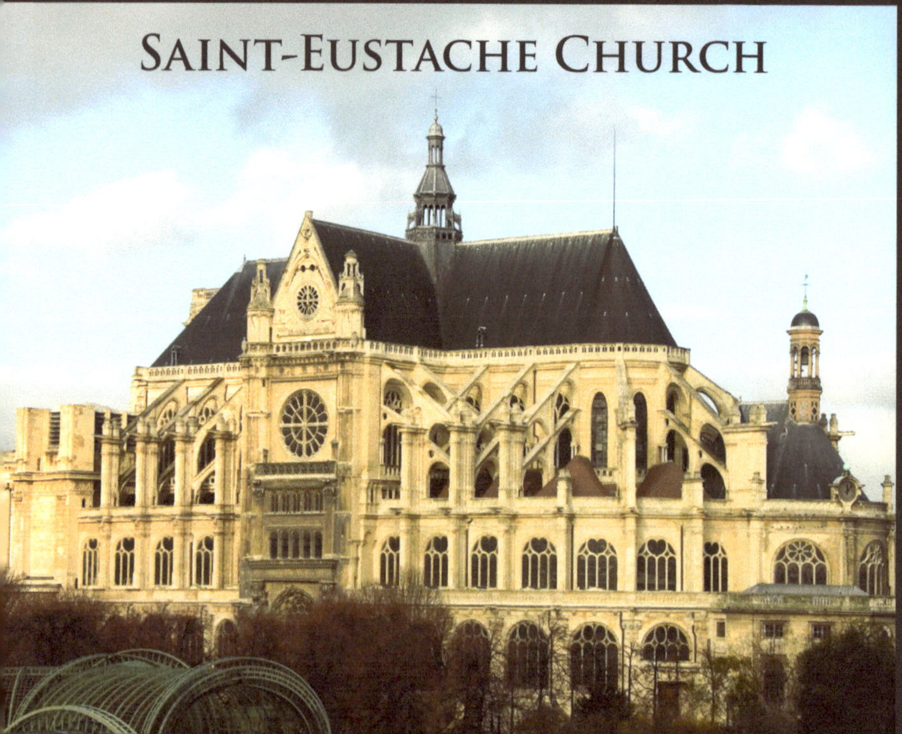

Saint-Eustache Church

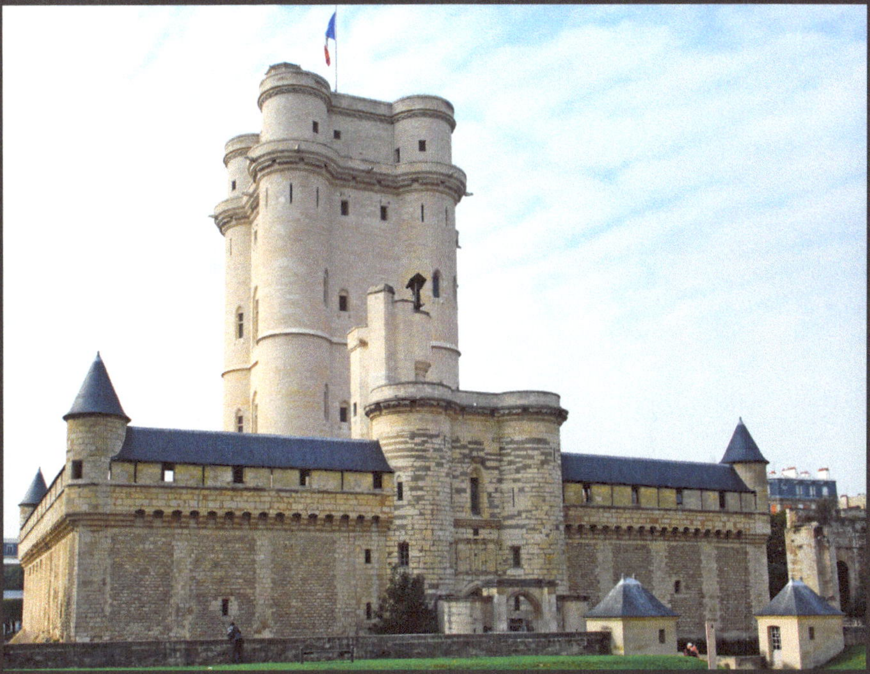

Vincennes Castle

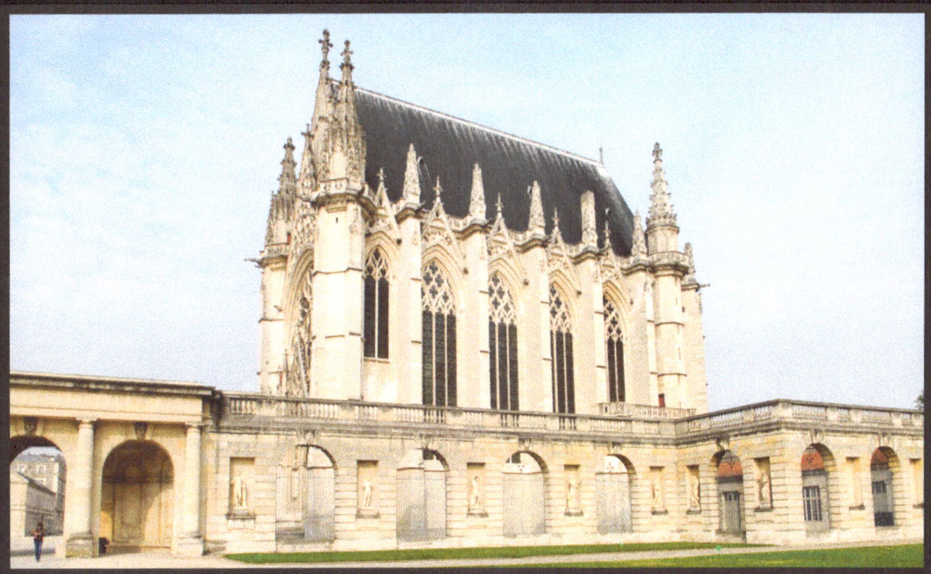

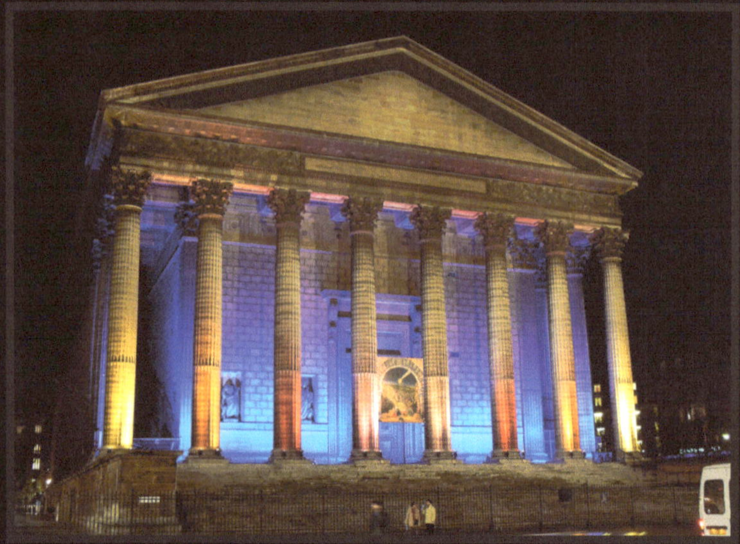

La Madeleine

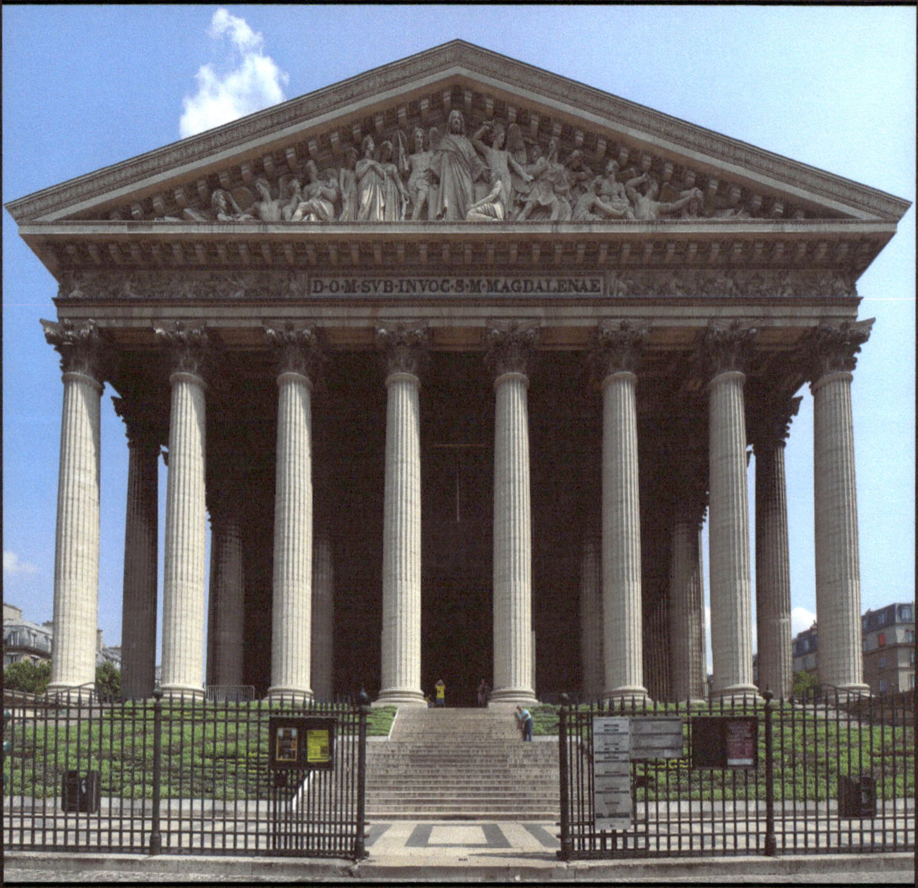

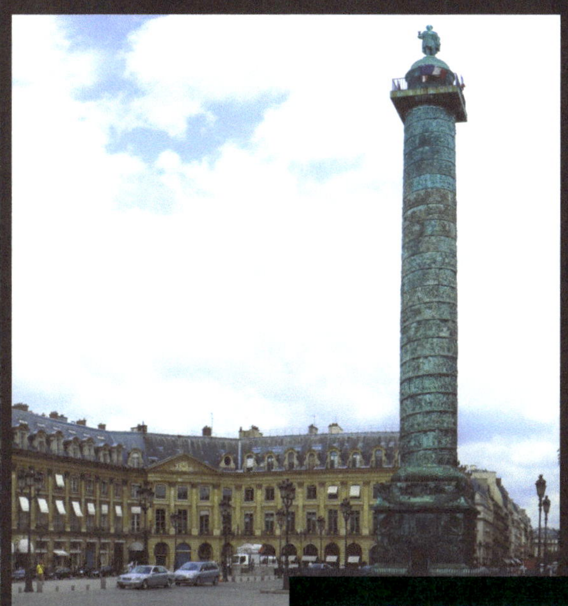

Vendome Square

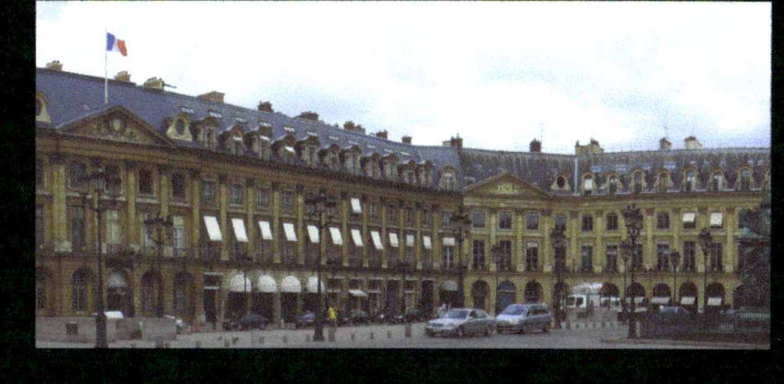

Arc du Carrousel

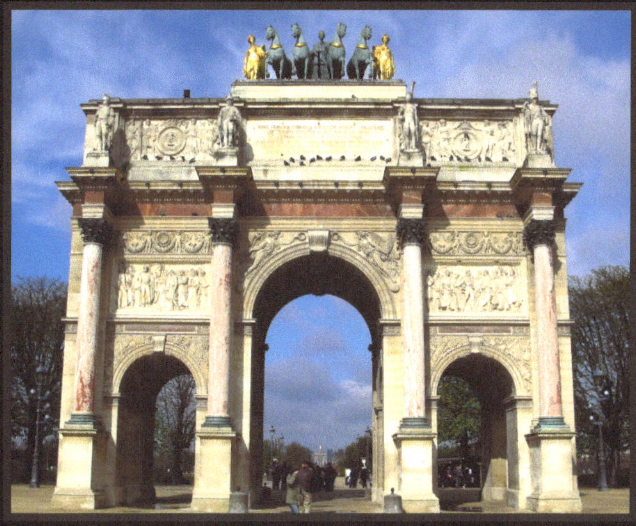

Aeiral View of Paris

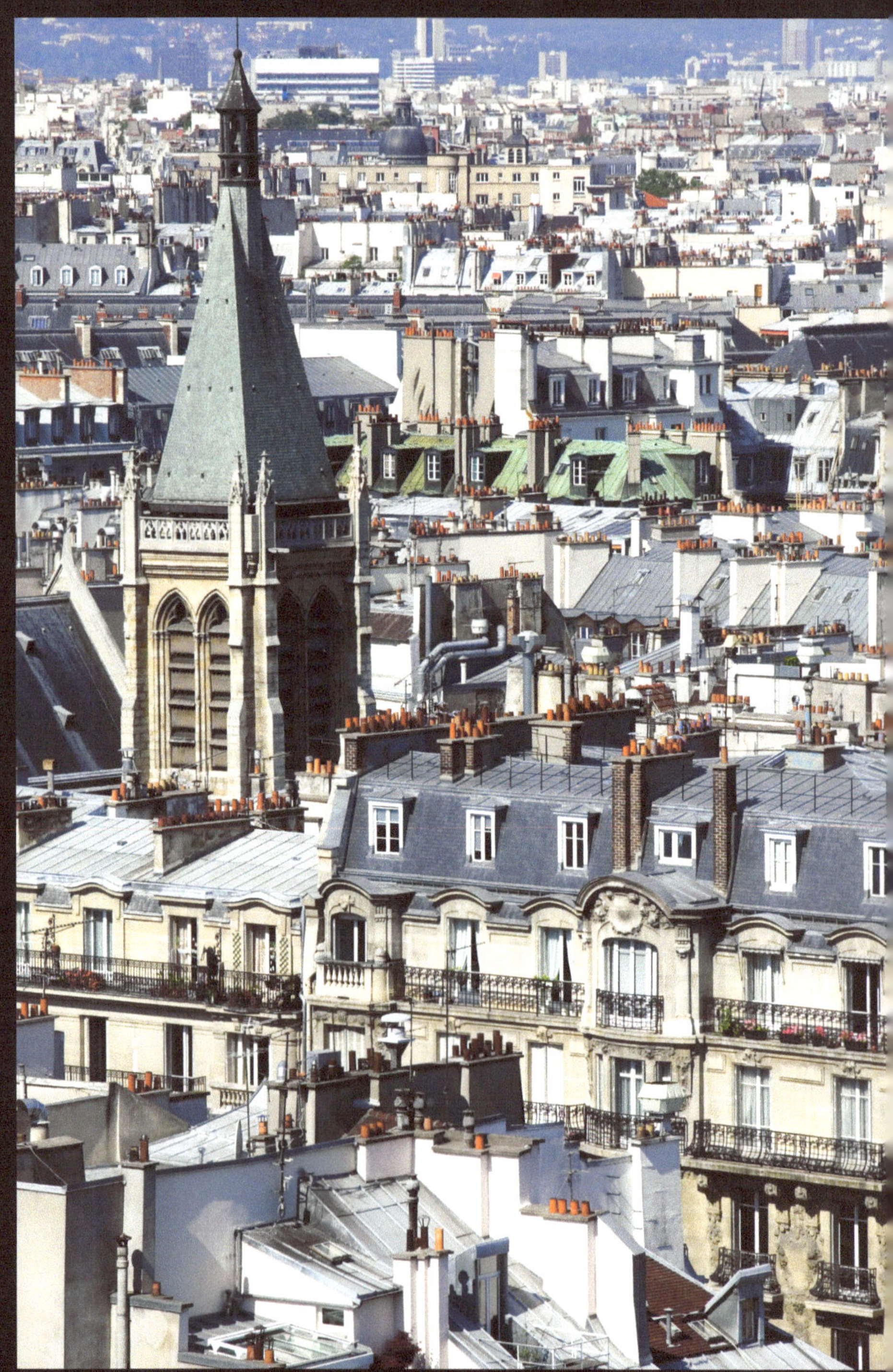

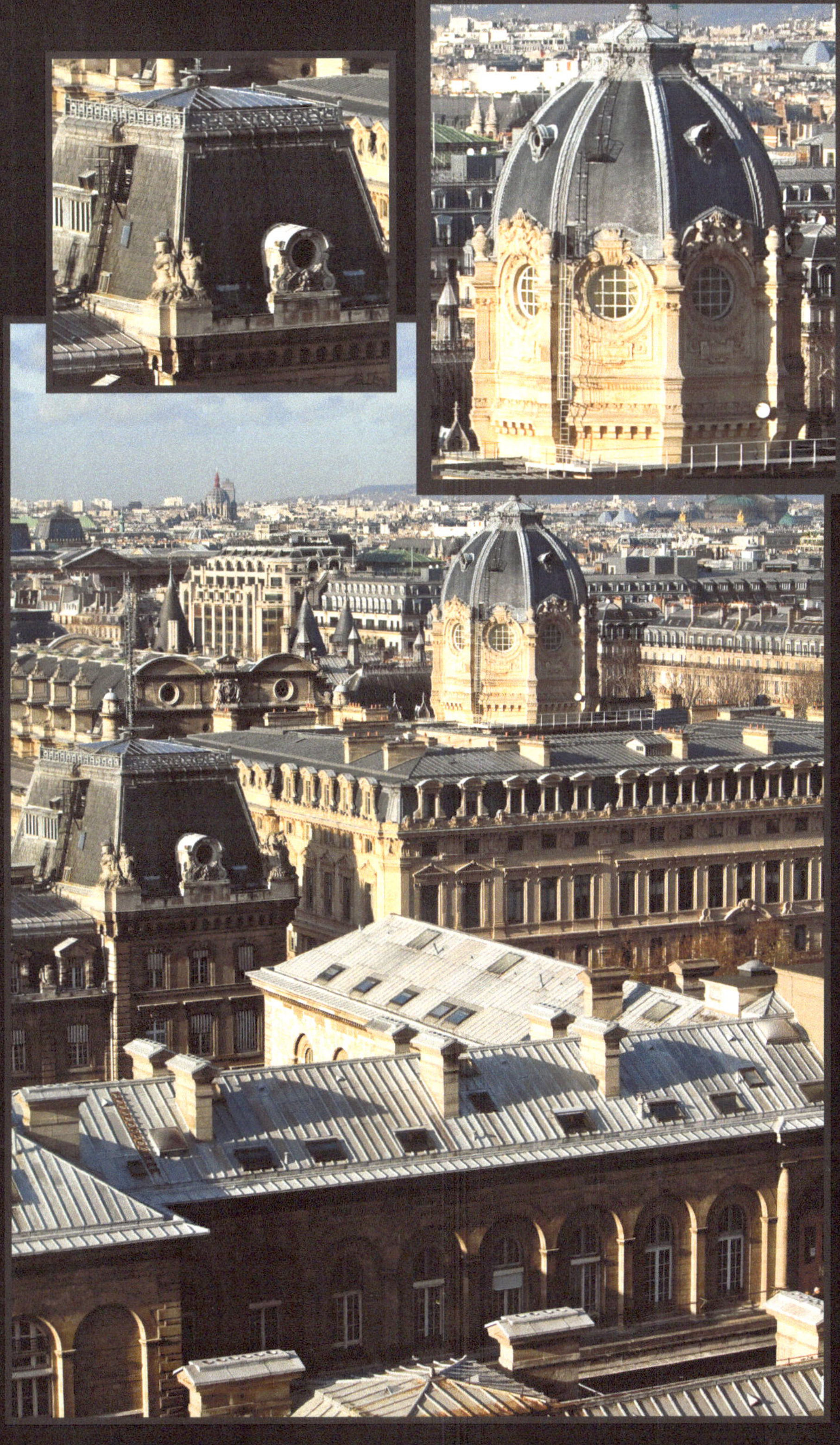

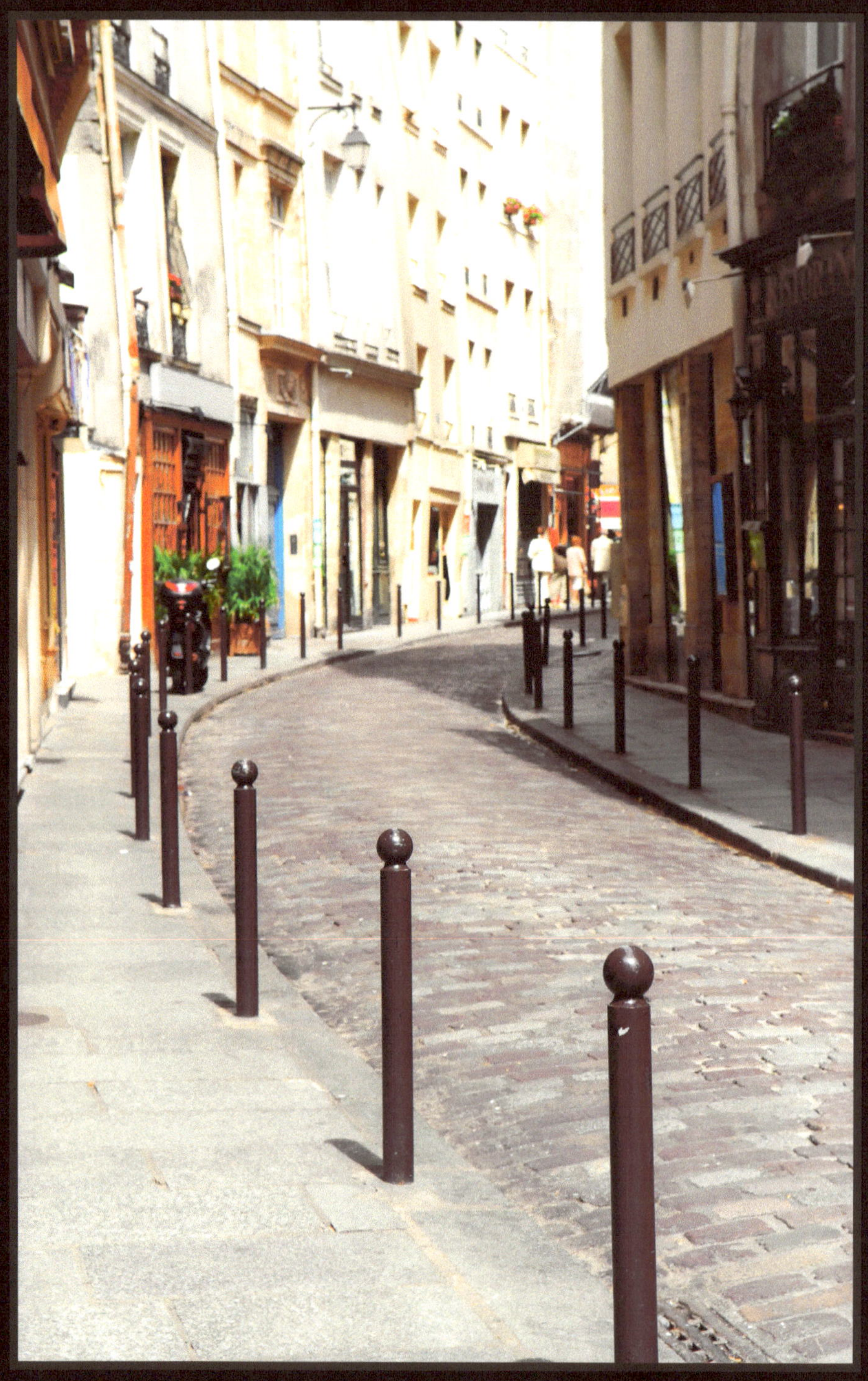

PARISIAN STREETS

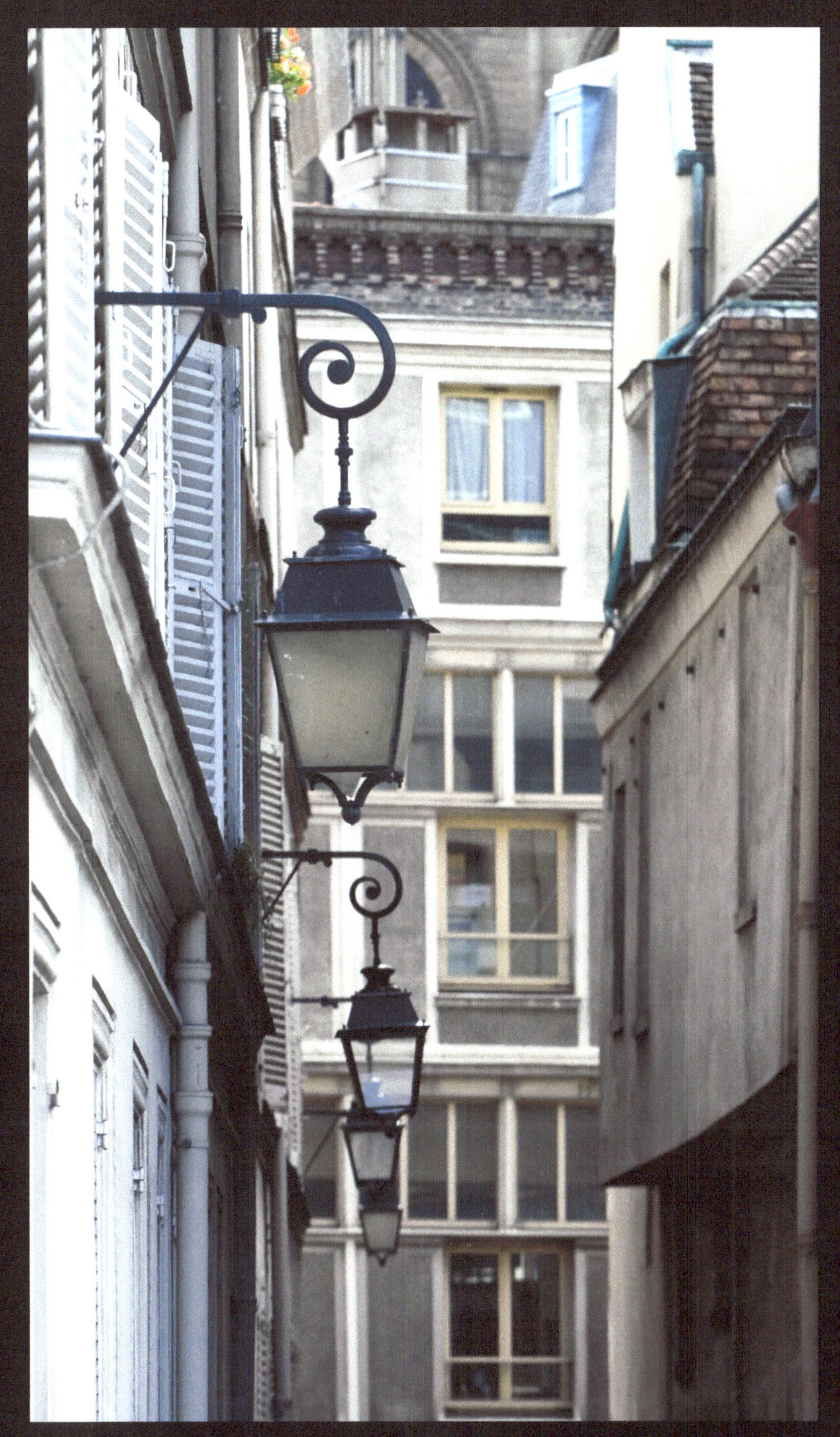

Parisian Architecture

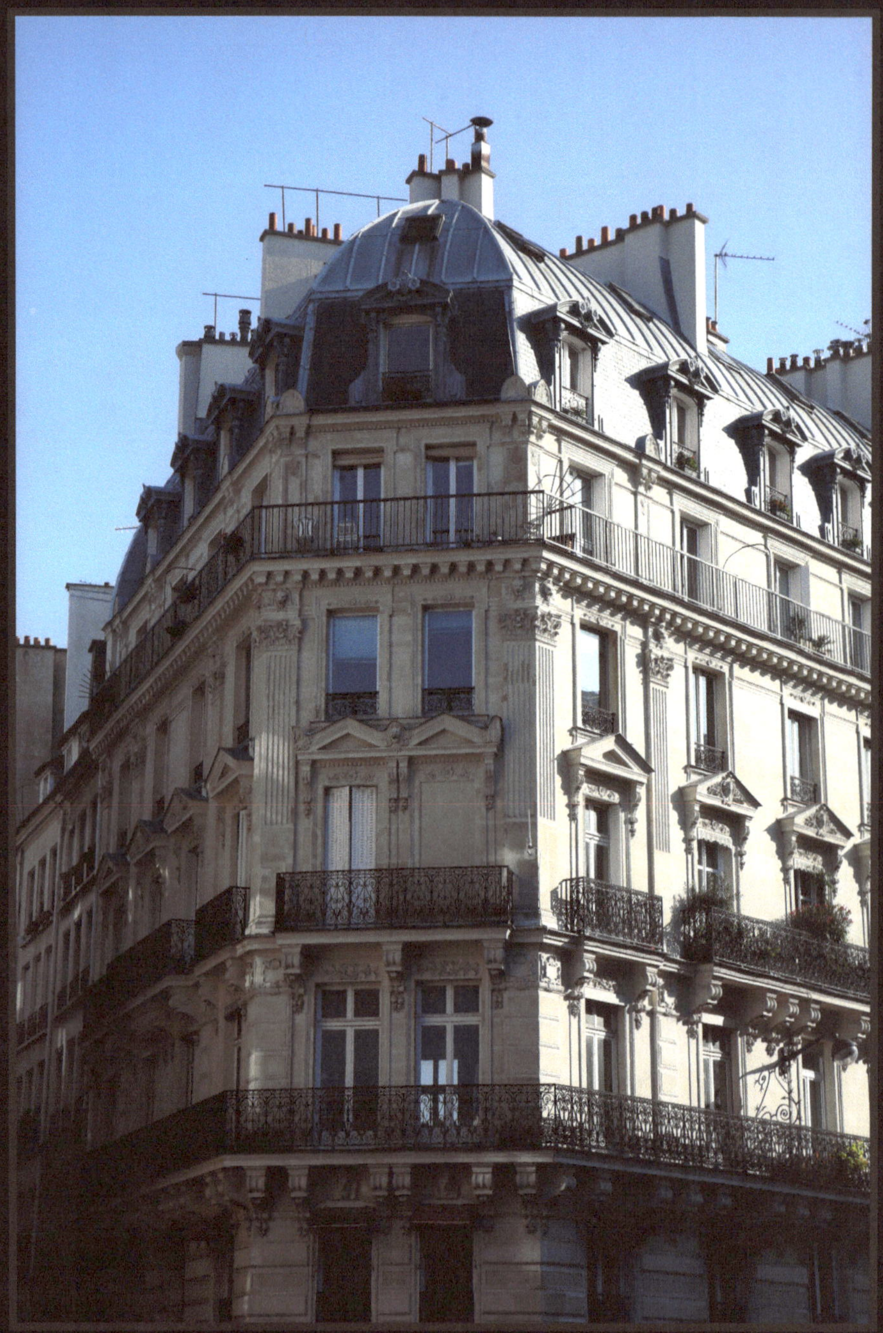

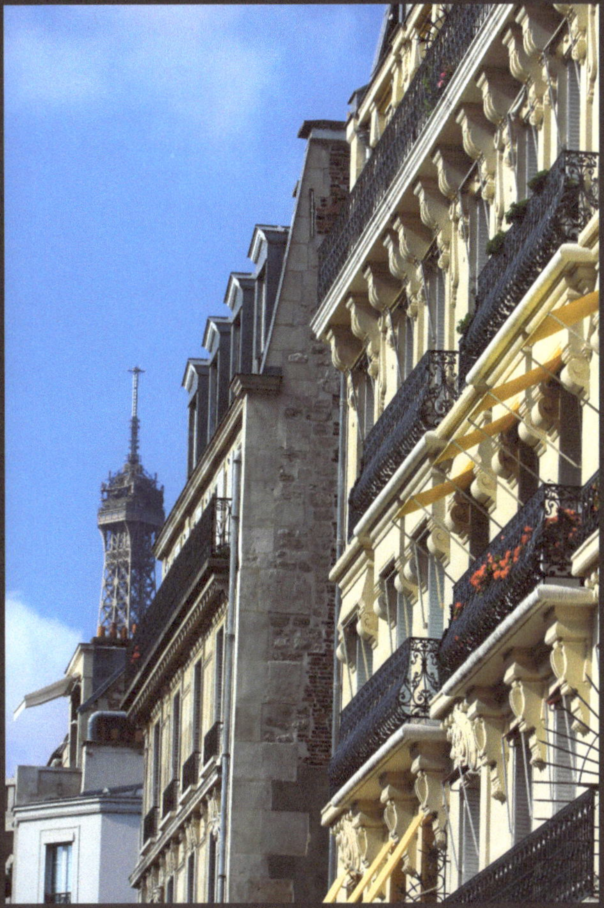

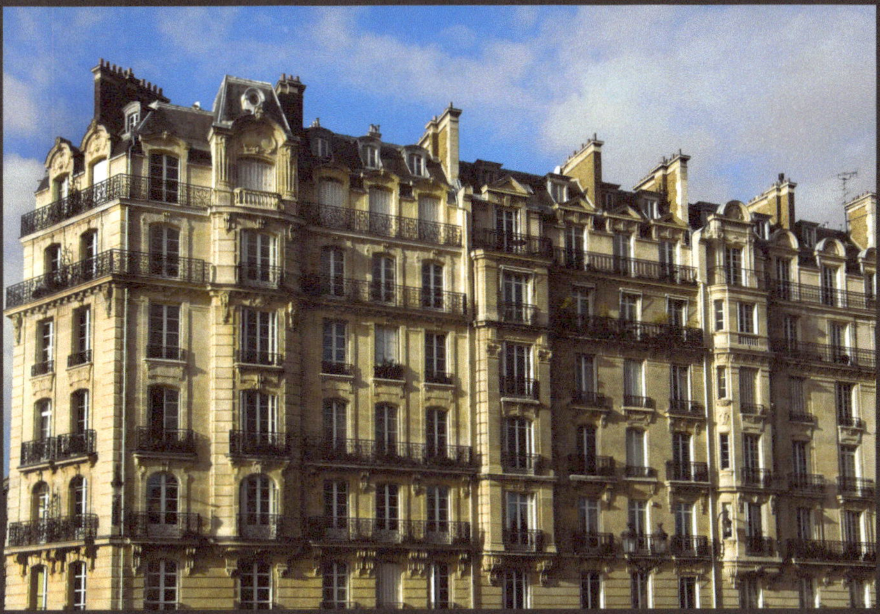

City Apartments

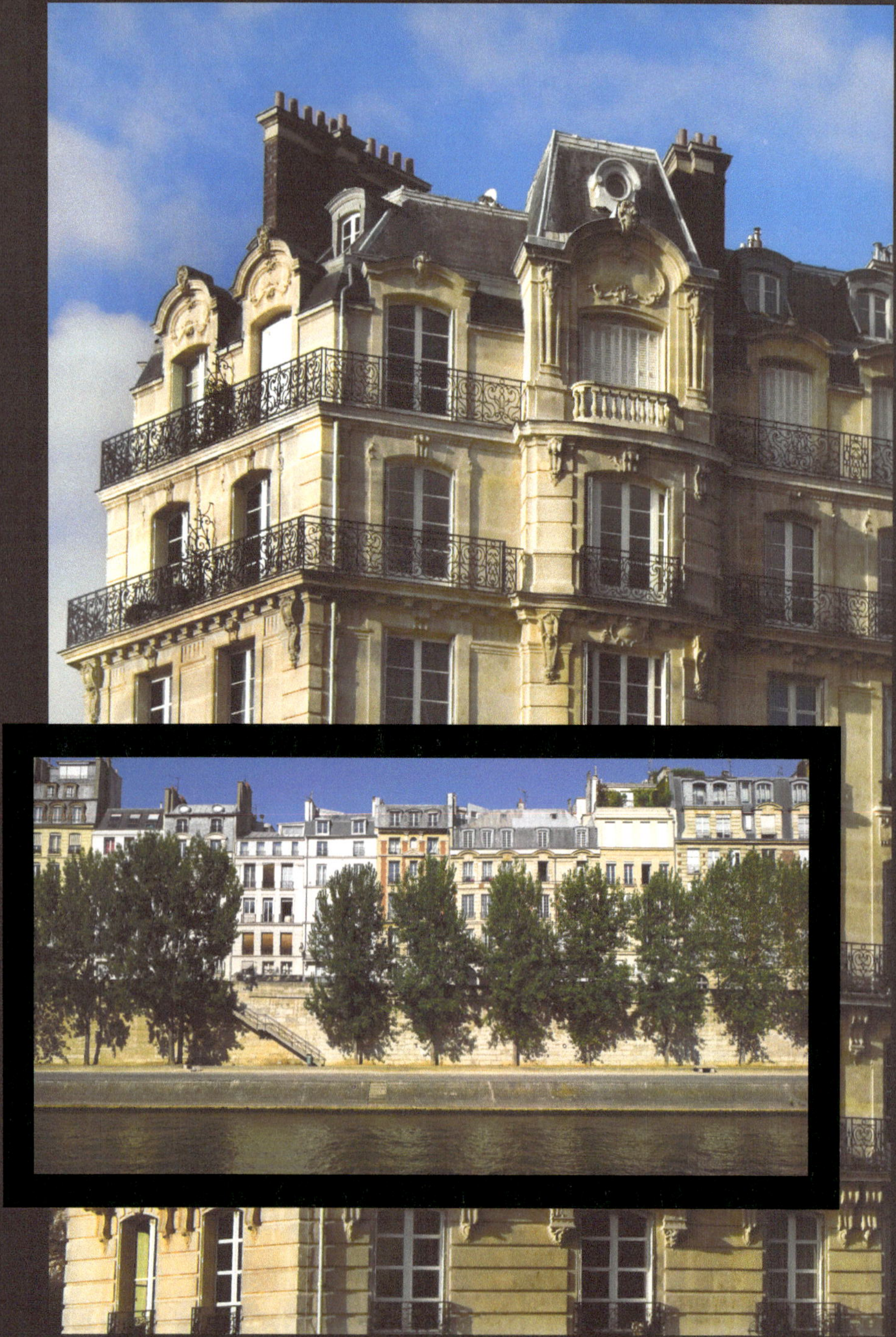

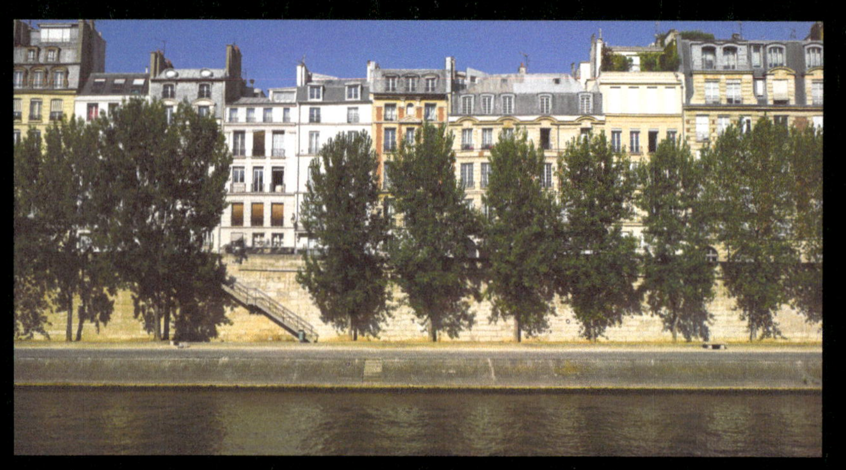

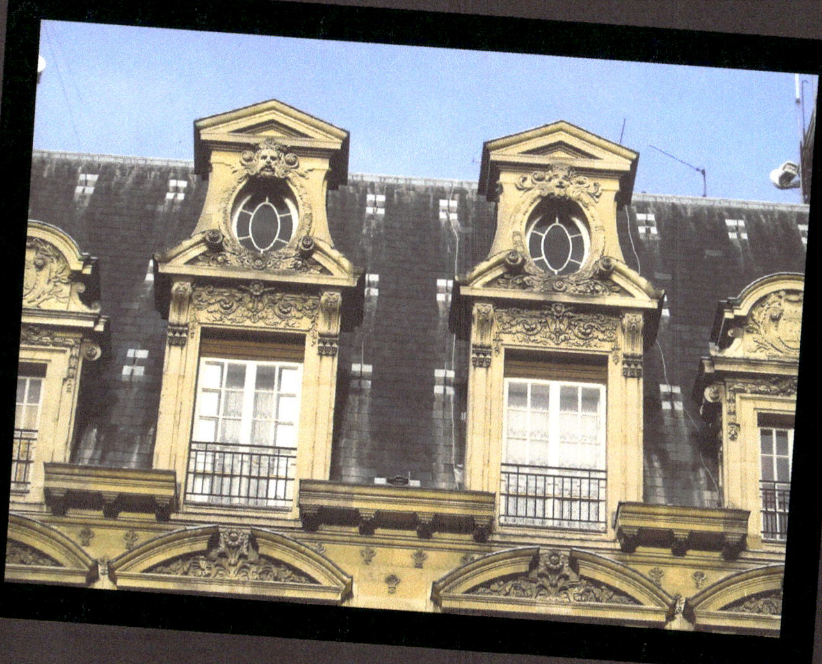

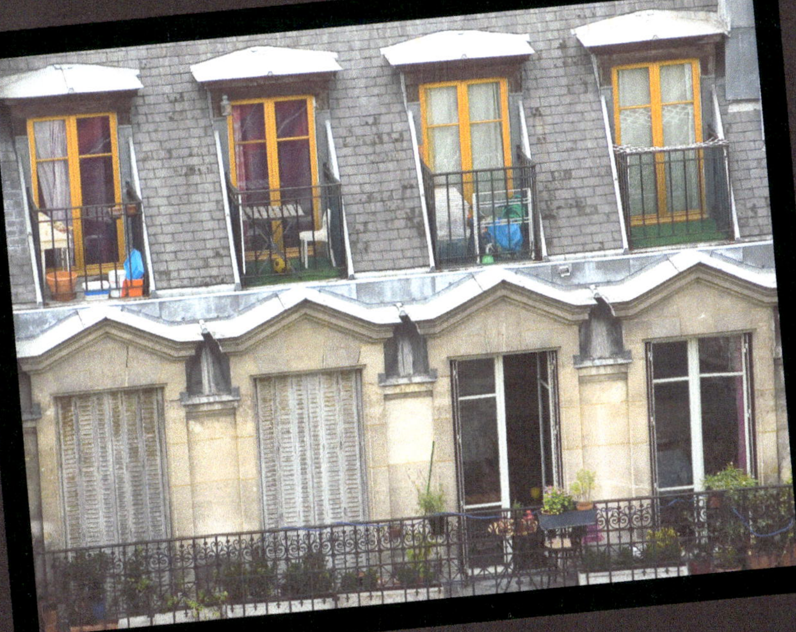

FLOWERS

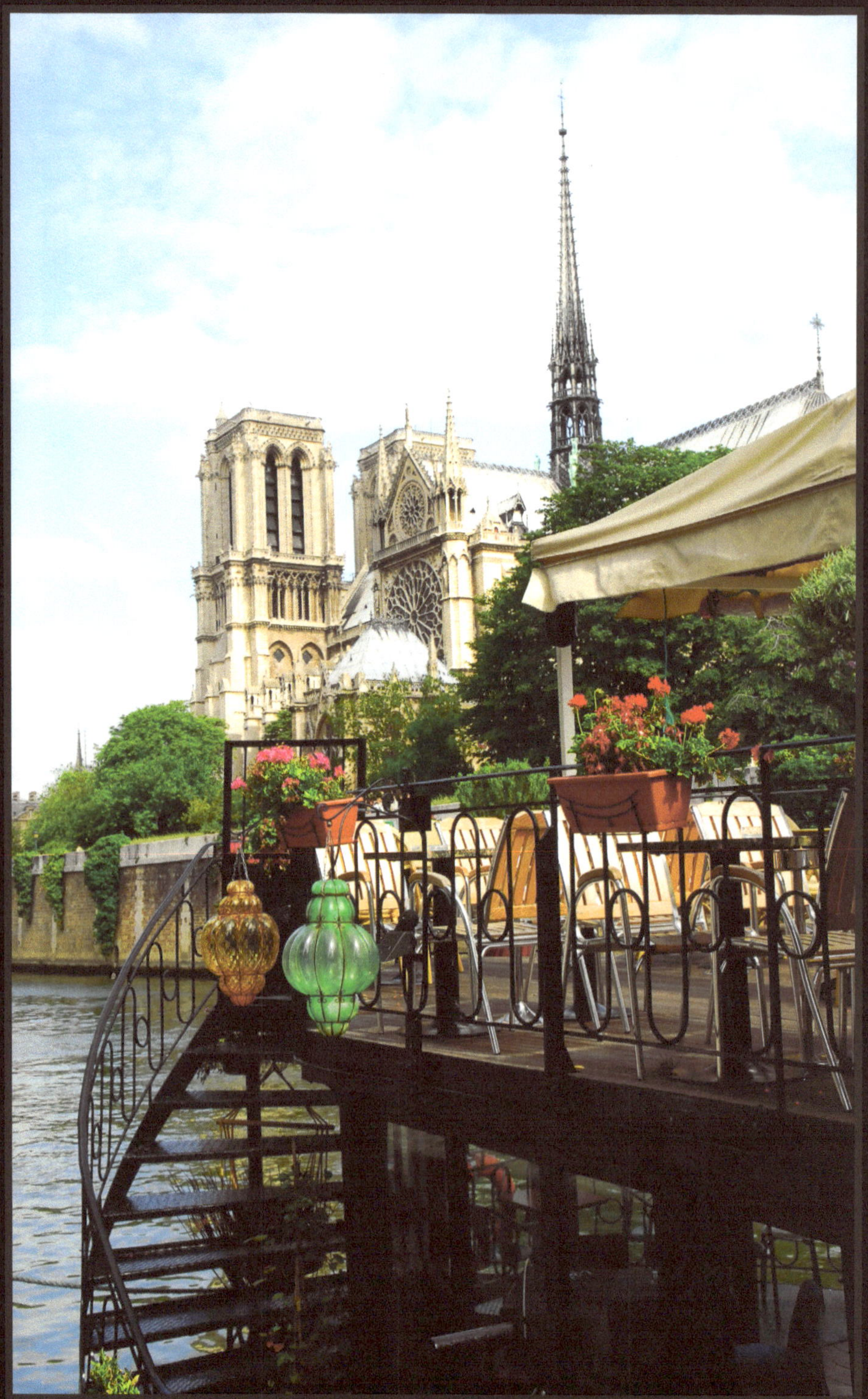

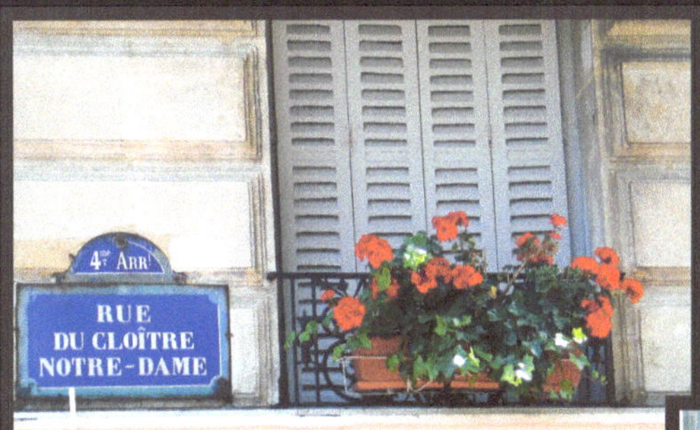
4E ARR
RUE
DU CLOÎTRE
NOTRE-DAME

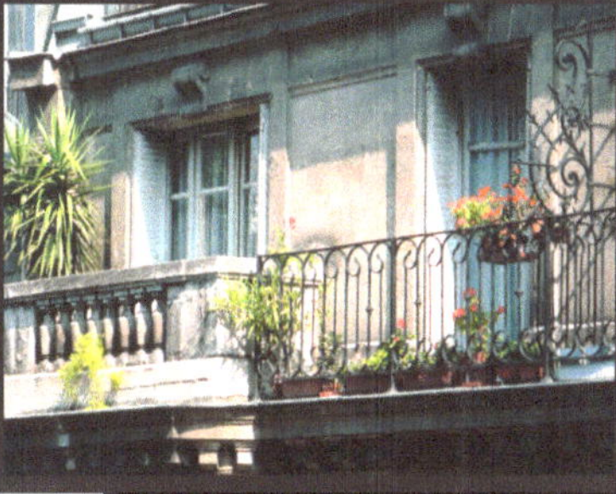

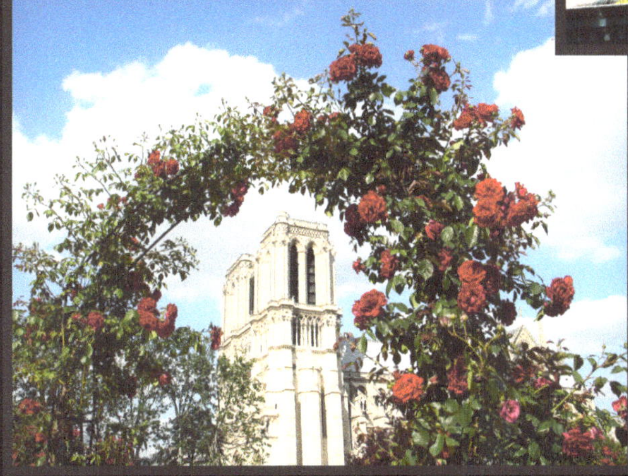

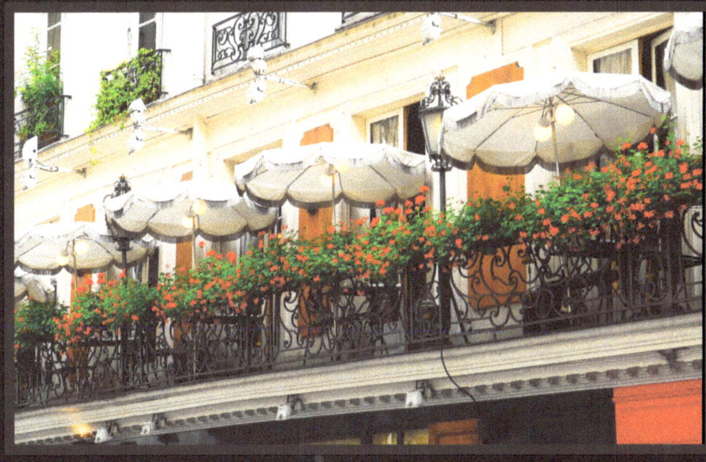

GREEN PARIS

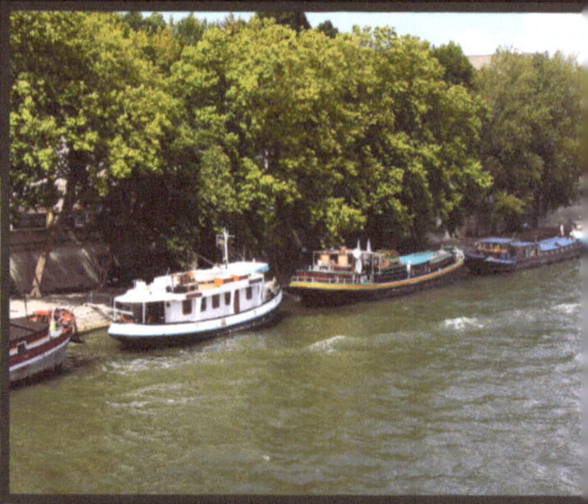

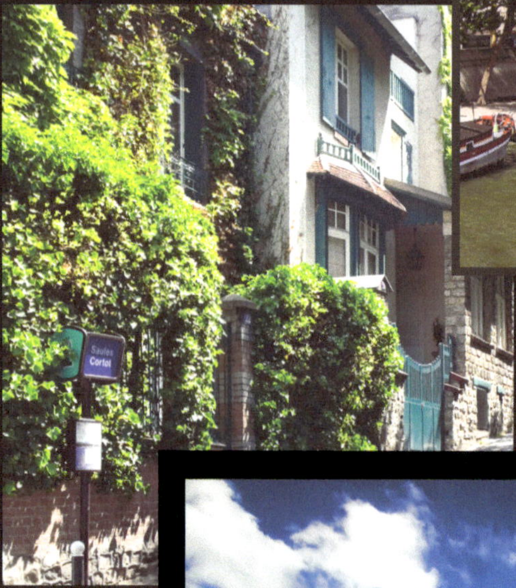

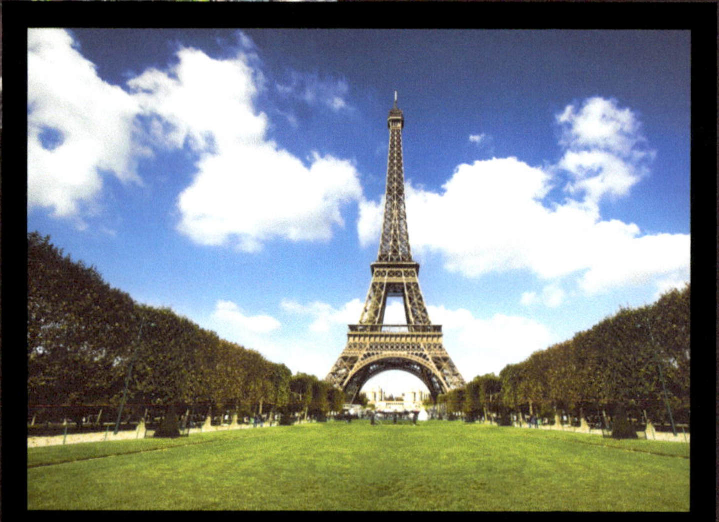

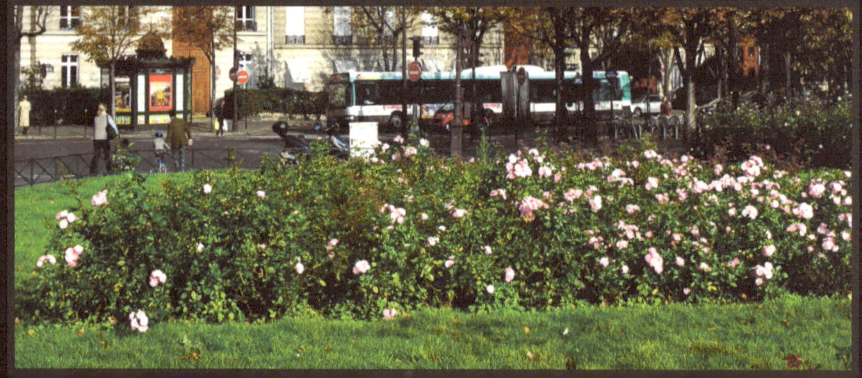

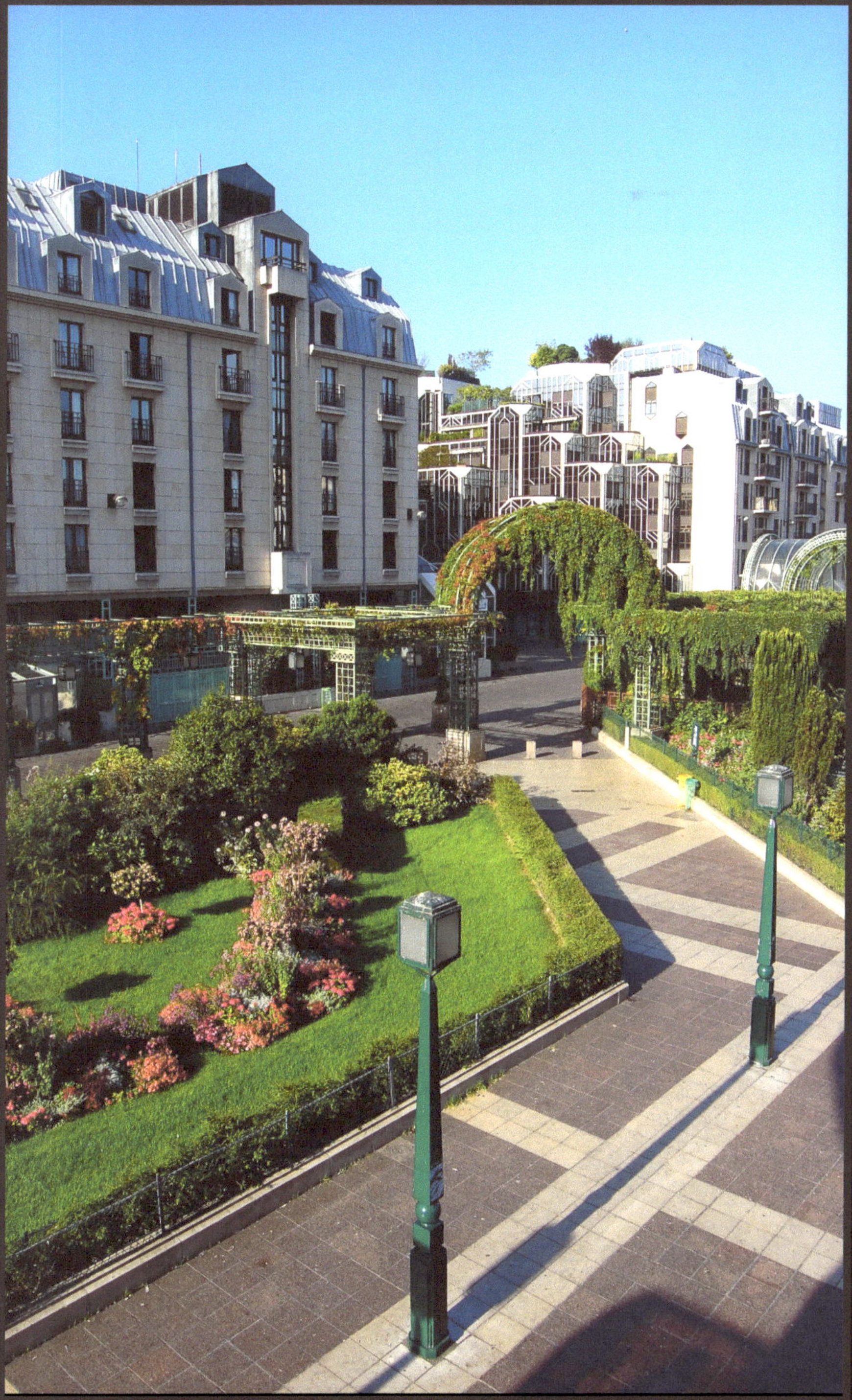

www.ingramcontent.com/pod-product-compliance
Lightning Source LLC
LaVergne TN
LVHW052257100826
845147LV00001B/75

* 9 7 8 0 9 8 6 6 0 0 4 8 7 *